Twentysomethings Talk About *The Woman I Am Becoming*

* * *

"Many questions do arise in my mind daily about what kind of person I am going to be...I know this book will be uplifting and comforting for every lady who reads it."

—BRITTNEY HENNIGSEN,
TWENTYSOMETHING STUDENT

"*The Woman I Am Becoming* wrestles with tough issues and wins!...Candid, Christ-centered, and captivating, Suzie's book...will be a resource for young women of all backgrounds. Add it to your bedroom library, girls!"

—STACIE RUTH STOELTING,
TWENTYSOMETHING AUTHOR, SPEAKER, AND SINGER
WWW.BRIGHTLIGHTMINISTRY.COM

"Sparkling, humble, wise, and complete...Guides the twentysomething woman on how to reconcile herself with her God and her world."

—MEAGAN STEPHENS,
TWENTYSOMETHING STUDENT

* * *

What others are saying about *The Woman I Am Becoming*

* * *

"Like all great mentors, Eller manages to create a safe place of acceptance—*and* issues a challenging call to follow Jesus at the same time. She respects the culture of twentysomethings, understands the confusion many feel, and shows how God alone can lead us through the dangerous, exciting adventure of transformation."

—**Mitali Perkins**,
author of *First Daughter: Extreme American Makeover* (Dutton, June 2007)

"Wow, is this a much-needed book! Since I, like most women, ventured into my twentysomething and married years far from home and the influence of older women who had been around the block, I so appreciate Suzanne's heart to create a way for young women to gather and receive that sort of input and counsel."

—**Shaunti Feldhahn**,
author of *For Women Only* and
coauthor of *For Young Women Only*

"The secrets shared here will make you beautiful from the inside out so you can become the truest definition of a 'Super (role) Model.'"

—**Tammy Bennett**,
author of *101 MakeOver Minutes* and
Looking Good from the Inside Out

"Eller has her finger on the pulse of the next generation. Any woman struggling with identity or her place in this world will benefit from this valuable resource."

—**Colin Creel**,
author of *Perspectives: A Spiritual Life Guide for Twentysomethings*
www.ColinCreel.com

"Suzie is see-through transparent with her readers and invites us to get real too...a gut-level honest book! I'm ordering copies for my daughters, ages 22 and 25."

—**Julie Garmon**,
blogger and speaker to teens and twentysomethings

"Today's young women are hungry for human connection and spiritual direction from women they can trust and respect. Suzanne Eller's gentle advice and admonitions give females hope in an increasingly narcissistic and competitive world."

—**Shirin Taber,**
Speaker and author of *Wanting All the Right Things* (Relevant, 2006)

"In a world where most twentysomethings are seeking advice from *Cosmo* and role models are few and far between, it's refreshing to know this book exists. It's real, raw, and relatable—a must-read for women from all backgrounds trying to figure out this thing called 'life.'"

—**Kerri Pomarolli,**
"Clean Female Comedian"
www.kerripom.com

"Transitioning into adulthood has many facets, and Suzie walks you through each one with biblical instruction, practical advice, and a tender understanding of where you may find yourself...You will feel like she is your personal mentor."

—**Denise A. Roberts**
ChristLIFE Ministries, Inc.
www.Christlife-ministries.com

"...Today's cookbook for being the woman God supports you in being and that you *truly* are...Suzanne offers delicious insight into how to fully embrace womanhood with truth, light, and love."

—**Christine Hassler,**
Life coach and author of *20-Something, 20-Everything*

"Responding with wisdom to questions posed by twentysomething women and asking a few of her own, Suzanne tackles tough topics like adult friendships and fitting in, singleness and waiting, serving others...and most importantly, strengthening your relationship with the Creator."

—**Zanese Duncan,**
Mom of twentysomethings and moms' prayer group leader

The Woman I Am Becoming

T. Suzanne Eller

HARVEST HOUSE PUBLISHERS
EUGENE, OREGON

Cover by Left Coast Design, Portland, Oregon

Cover photo © LWA / The Image Bank / Getty Images

T. Suzanne Eller is published in association with Books & Such Literary Agency, 52 Mission Circle, Suite 122, PMB 170, Santa Rosa, CA 95409-5370.

THE WOMAN I AM BECOMING

Published by Harvest House Publishers
Eugene, Oregon 97402
www.harvesthousepublishers.com

Eller, T. Suzanne.
The woman I am becoming / T. Suzanne Eller.
p. cm.
Includes bibliographical references.
ISBN-13: 978-0-7369-2030-8
ISBN-10: 0-7369-2030-7
Christian-women—Religious life. 2. Christian women—Conduct of life. 3. Women—Psychology. I. Title.
BV4527.E437 2007
248.8'43—dc22

2007002512

Printed in the United States of America

07 08 09 10 11 12 13 14 15 / VP-SK / 10 9 8 7 6 5 4 3 2 1

To Kimberly Gilles-Marshall,
my niece and my friend

ACKNOWLEDGMENTS

Writing a book is always difficult. But as I wrote this I got to hang out with a group of my favorite twentysomethings, which made it fun. I want to give a huge hug to Melissa, Tiffany, Angie, Megan, Sarah G., Sarah B., Shawna, Jess, Katie, Jamie, Michelle, Annie, Shermona, Nichole, and Raychelle. Thank you for your honesty. Thanks for your insight. I loved our conversations and am grateful they will continue. You guys simply rock!

Thank you to my agent, Janet Grant, for believing in me. You know my heart, and you know how badly I desire to minister. You know my future dreams, and you continue to guide me with diligence and grace.

I want to thank my church family at M1A. I can't imagine doing this without your prayers and encouragement. It means more than you'll ever know. Thanks to Pastor Steve for celebrating each new book with me.

Thank you to my gorgeous husband, Richard, and my beautiful adult children, Leslie, Melissa, Ryan, Josh, and Stephen. You are my heart. Thank you, Josh and Richard, for reading several chapters and giving feedback, though this is a book for women.

I want to thank Paul Gossard, and the rest of the Harvest House team. When you invited me to join the HH family as an author, I felt at home. What a privilege to be a part of your ministry!

CONTENTS

Let's create a village

"UNLESS YOU LIVE IN A VILLAGE somewhere in the third world, gone are the days when mothers, cousins, aunts, grandmothers, and female mentors huddled together at the hearth, giving loving and supportive advice about marriage, motherhood, community life, and pursuit of vocational dreams."[1]

Many twentysomethings agree with those words written by Shirin Taber, saying they live in a disconnected society. In our autonomous world it is possible to connect with people from all over the globe, but real and deep relationships take a lot of effort. Perhaps you too are finding it difficult to locate a strong nucleus of women where you can share your hopes, dreams, and frustrations.

Your 20s are an exciting and lonely period. As I travel and talk with beautiful young women from all over the continent, I sense a growing need and desire for true community. Shirin Taber agrees in her book, *Wanting All the Right Things:*

> We need each other more than ever. Many of us grew up as latchkey kids, come from broken homes, or weren't taught to plan or prioritize for the difficult crossroads we find ourselves facing today. Our baby-boomer mothers and fathers, influenced by the sexual revolution, have in many respects only added to our confusion.

> They've taught us to mistrust men, become economically self-reliant, indulge our anger, and pursue independence—at any cost.[2]

I don't know what influences you have in your life, but I can look back at the past 25 years and see clearly how older women influenced me. Many stepped in at crucial times in my life and modeled faith to me. They gently advised, or perhaps they only listened as I worked through issues on my own, but that was enough. None of these women had all the answers or pretended to know what I needed in my life, but they shared what they had learned along the way. These women impacted my life.

You and I can also learn from each other. These past few months as I've tossed out ideas and thoughts to my twentysomething friends, I've loved hearing their insights. The depth of their comments, and their honesty about issues, helped me stay on track. We talked about what they say matters right now in their life. As time passed we found we had more in common than we realized, no matter our ages or differences.

That's why I even dare to present *The Woman I Am Becoming* to you. Please consider this book a form of community, a group of strong women talking about identity, relationships, faith, and the future. This is the biblical model of womanhood—women of all ages coming together to encourage each other, to talk frankly, to pray for each other, and to connect right where we are.

And it can also mold a conversation between you and God. As you read, you'll have an opportunity to take the issues deeper with questions at the end of each chapter. I pray that you invite the one who loves you best—God—into these one-on-ones.

Are you excited to begin this journey? Let's do it!

PART ONE: IDENTITY

Who you are becoming

What you say about yourself means nothing in God's work.
It's what God says about you that makes the difference.
FROM 2 CORINTHIANS 10

Blog

I'm not a clone...

Current mood: perplexed

I have been struggling with the image of what a REAL woman of God should be like. There are women I respect, and I see things in each of them that I like and want in my own life. But I also see things that I dislike and strive not to copy. The real question for me is, *What do I want to be?* Well, I want to be a leader who takes initiative. I love music and want to lead people to worship God. I want to be happy. I want to be strong. But I have so many questions, like,

Who will I marry?

What does God want to do in my life?

Where will destiny take me, and how far can I go?

Will I be a good wife or a good mother one day?

How do I know when and how to take the next step?

I'm young, but I've faced so many things in my past that I wonder if I even want children or if I'll succeed in a relationship. I know I'm supposed to figure all of this out on my own, but I want God to direct me. My words. My thoughts. My decisions. My actions. I need him to help me take the right steps toward my future husband and career. I need God's direction in every aspect of my life.

I want to be a REAL woman of God, whatever that means.

Raychelle Kappell, twentysomething

ONE

Woman under construction?

THERE WEREN'T ANY FIREWORKS. No sparkling lights dazzled me from the sky. It was an ordinary Sunday morning. Ordinary, except for the fact that I heard from God.

Is that you, Lord?

My stomach rumbled. Maybe it was actually the pizza buffet I'd enjoyed the night before. I don't know about you, but it seems to me that audible conversations with God happened much more frequently in the Old Testament than they do in our modern world. There were no burning bushes that Sunday morning,[1] and yet somehow I knew it was God. I knew because the words were quiet and deep on the inside of me, and they were words I would never say to myself:

Stand in front of me as the woman you are becoming.

If you had viewed me through the eyes of others, you would have seen a strong, faith-filled, twentysomething woman. In many ways, I *was* that person. I loved God. I believed my life mattered. But I often related to God, and to other people, as if I were in limbo. I appeared confident, but I lacked direction. I was truly happy as a young wife and mother, but as a person I was at a crossroads. I was privately asking a myriad of questions, like, *What's next? Do I have something to offer others? Where are you taking me, God? How will I know which way to go?* Those questions seemed insurmountable. I hoped I would recognize the next step in womanhood when I stumbled over it. When I looked in the mirror I didn't see a full-fledged woman. I saw me—a woman under construction. A building project that was dragging on and on, complete with breakdowns and cost overruns.

That morning I stood in the sanctuary thanking God. My praise was sincere, but I was talking to him from the heart of the person I saw in the mirror, rather than as the creation God viewed as his own. My friends and I were from different backgrounds and in differing stages of life. We talked about the unique issues of identity. My personal battle came from growing up in chaos and dysfunction, and I talked to God as if I were still in need of rescue, still needing to be fixed, when what I really needed was direction and empowerment. Very few knew of the inner struggle to find my way, except for those who loved me best.

God was one of those.

That quiet voice inside of me spoke with loving authority. It was time to view Suzie Eller in a whole new way. I could see all my doubts, fear, and uncertainty, mixed with growing enthusiasm, faith, and hope. God was asking me to refocus so I could see opportunities ahead with my name on them. God held the blueprints with my design and my future in his hands. He knew my past. He knew what had shaped me. He saw the wispy cracks of fear and doubt in my foundation. He saw my strengths, such as compassion and the desire to share my faith with others who might not understand or embrace faith. He saw my desire to be all that I could be with his help.

I saw my life as a construction zone. All I could perceive was the dust and noise and sweat. But God—the ultimate designer of my life—reached down to remind me that he had plans for me. It was time to view myself in an entirely different way: *As the woman I was becoming.*

Transform me

> *Grace gives me the freedom to be who God designed me to be.*
>
> Rebecca Barlow Jordan,
> fiftysomething author of *At Home in My Heart*

In *Every Thought Captive,* Jerusha Clark describes the process of transformation.

> We can't always tell that we are being transformed because our vision is not like God's. Unlimited by time, he can view us as we are and as we will be. His perception of us is not based on isolated moments, nor does he see us only against the backdrop of our past. Instead, God knows who we are right now—a new creation—and who we are becoming.[2]

In theory, transformation sounds like a wonderful thing. It is a word that produces images of butterflies and beauty. But transformation is actually more like road construction. It's messy and slow, and it can be unnerving. Not long ago, I was driving to Dallas to see my daughter. The normally wide-open freeway was torn up for nearly 60 miles. I gripped the wheel as four lanes narrowed to two. Huge semis blocked me in like a sedan sandwich. Orange safety cones, temporary concrete barriers, and bumper-to-bumper traffic put my teeth on edge. I looked for exit signs. *Better to take the back roads than continue like this,* I thought. But there were no good options. I was relieved when the construction zone ended and I could zip down the highway once again.

All I could see were the obstacles, and yet that 60-mile stretch was in the process of transformation. At the end of the project was a smooth ride, and construction was necessary for that to occur. The mess and dust and even the apprehension were all part of the process.

Your construction is much the same. You see the obstacles. You might feel the discomfort. And perhaps, at times, you want to hit the exit road and just cruise for a while, or skip over the process and take what feels good right now—even if the payback down the road isn't what you want. But I hope you will view transformation in a different light. We are all works in progress, and God's handiwork is emerging in each of our lives. There is a plan for you. As you enter the next phase (whatever that may be), think about these three principles:

1. Transformation isn't always easy.
2. You won't always feel fully prepared.
3. You don't have to do it alone.

Shouldn't this be easier?

Perhaps the biggest tall tale shared in the Christian world is that when you become a believer, life will suddenly be magical and work out perfectly. You pray and—poof—you receive a new car. Or if you give, money falls from heaven.

I know that God blesses us, and I'm grateful for all I have because of him, but it rarely has anything to do with new cars or cash. The reality is, Jesus *suffered* while he was on earth. He and those who followed his teachings changed the world, and along the way they experienced humiliation, persecution, and challenges. But his life wasn't tragic; it was abundant. The blessings Jesus and the disciples received had nothing to do with their finances or where they laid their head at night, but rather with their contentment and adventure as they experienced God's plan firsthand. They were on the right path even in the painful and challenging moments of daily living.

Their faith remained genuine in spite of the difficult times. The peace they experienced could not be taken from them because it did not depend on feelings or conditions.

As you are transformed into the person God knew from the

very beginning, you'll find joy and purpose in your faith. But there will be times you question God, and that's okay. God isn't afraid of your doubts, and turning to him when things don't make sense is a smart move.

When bad things happen

Tiffany Hammonds had life figured out. She married Kris. She was in college, studying to be a teacher. She had a close relationship with her family, especially her mother, Leann. One cold February day Leann became seriously ill. The diagnosis was cancer. After a few treatments, the family was encouraged by a positive report. But one night they were all shocked when Leann passed away unexpectedly.

Tiffany's life changed in a matter of moments.

She grieved the loss of her mom, who was her best friend. She struggled as her family was redefined. She continued to love and to live, but the loss of her mom didn't go away. It wasn't a road she chose to walk, but she discovered that her faith was her strength even when she was most angry with God. She found comfort in the promise that God would always be with her, and that he wouldn't give up on her or leave her.[3]

> "When my mom passed away, I felt I had to grow up so fast. I needed to be strong and have my life figured out. I'm not saying this for sympathy, but I didn't know what to do. I didn't know if God was really there. The person I confided in, questioned all the time, and looked up to as a REAL woman of God was no longer with me. It was a total curveball."
>
> Tiffany Hammonds, twentysomething

Unexpected suffering may make you question transformation. *Am I on the right path? Why did this happen?* It might be the loss of someone you love, but it also can be a dream slipping out of your fingers, or the disintegration of a relationship you treasure.

On Tuesday, April 20, 1999, at Columbine High School in Littleton, Colorado, two teenage students went on a shooting rampage, killing 12 fellow students and a teacher and wounding 24 others. In this deadliest school shooting in United States history, Crystal Miller is a survivor. In her book *Marked for Life,* she says,

> Seems the greater the difficulty, the more prone we are to lean into God, tucking every fiber of our being into his strong chest. In those moments, we realize with fresh appreciation our lack of control, our lack of strength, our lack of steadiness, our lack of reasonable thought. We *need* him. And we need him desperately.[4]

Transformation often occurs in the messiest parts of our existence. It's not that God brings tragedy so that we might grow, but that we grasp true strength when we turn to something much larger than ourselves.

Transformation in the cleanup stage

Every Sunday morning I join several women—most in their 20s—in a class at my home church. A few of the women live in a residential rehabilitation clinic where they are finding help for substance abuse. One morning the students were asked to describe their life in a metaphor. Some said, "I'm a butterfly, for now I'm flying free." Others painted beautiful word pictures, but one took a deep breath. "My life has been a hurricane," she said. "I've hurt people and I've left a terrible aftermath. Now I'm in the cleanup stage and it's the hardest thing I've ever faced." She paused, wiping away a tear. "But I'm grateful to be in the cleanup stage."

"Why is that?" the teacher asked.

"Because it means I'm moving forward. I'm willing to stay in this stage as long as I need to."

This twentysomething is new in her faith, but she has already

grasped a powerful message. Sometimes the messes in our lives come from our own choices. It might seem easier to find an exit and skip the rebuilding phase, but there is transformation in the cleanup. Keri Wyatt Kent in the book *Listen* says,

> Somehow, I have ended up where I am, whether by God's intervention or my own choices, or other people's choices, or a blend of those things. Instead of complaining about where you are, notice it and say, "How did I get here?" "What can change and what can't?" "What about my life does God want to redeem?" "What does he want to accomplish in me, and in others, through my life's pain and challenges?"[5]

Becoming the woman you desire to be might go slower than you think it should as you repair relationships, forgive others and yourself, and carve out a whole new way of living. But I pray you'll take heart as you experience God's "grace mixed with faith and love poured over me and into me. And all because of Jesus."[6]

> "I cannot stop until I—for lack of a better word—conquer. I want to figure it all out."
>
> RAYCHELLE KAPPELL, TWENTYSOMETHING

When life hands you a challenge, or when you're ready to do a 180 to discover what God really has for you, this is part of the construction process. Often you need to complete the work in earlier phases before moving forward—but then, when you do so, it is with purpose, with knowledge to help you avoid the pitfalls that snagged you in the past, and with certainty that God has more for your life.

You may not quite feel ready

Transformation nudges us into the next phase of life so we can find our wings. Sounds poetic, doesn't it? Sure—unless you've seen a bird fly for the first time. Picture it with me: A fledgling bird with tufts of feathers is prodded to the edge of the nest. The nest is quite comfy. She's been content to eat minced worms, regurgitated into her beak like clockwork. But she's ready to fly, even though the ground seems a million miles away. The momma bird pushes her over the side and into the cold, cruel world. The baby bird plunges down in the air, every cartoon strip of Garfield with feathers hanging out of his mouth flashing before her eyes. And then the miracle happens.

She starts to fly.

Fly, baby, fly

Just like this not-so-picturesque scene, God is famous for nudging people out of insecurity and introducing them to destiny. He did so with Mary, Esther, Deborah, and others in the Bible. He did so with me. He's nudging you to discover his purpose as well.

> "I wonder how different it would be if I had been given a little bit more of a 'push' to spread my wings and fly."
>
> ANGIE YANDELL, TWENTYSOMETHING

One of the most famous encounters in the Bible occurred when Moses and God met in the wilderness.[7] Moses was comfortable in life, but God suggested, according to the blueprints, that it was time for him to become a powerful leader. Moses wasn't enthused with the idea, so he offered an excuse. "Lord, I stutter," he said, again and again.

God reminded Moses that he knew about his limitations but had handpicked him for this task. He didn't thrust him into the next phase without encouragement. He promised that he wouldn't lead alone, that God would be with him from that day forward.

I don't want to compare myself with Moses, but like Moses, my word from God that day in church wasn't an invitation. It was a consultation with God's creation, a reminder that there were great things ahead if I dared to fly. Moses argued with God, but the Creator stood firm. Not long after this conversation, Moses

went on to free a nation from slavery and oppression. That job was never easy, and there were many challenges through every phase. Strangely, his ability to communicate became crucial, as he negotiated the release of the Israelite people with the angry ruler of Egypt. It served him well when he was both leader and judge of thousands upon thousands of people. His life became an example as he learned to trust and obey God in spite of his doubts and his limitations.

Even when Moses failed, his failures were of a great man who expressed faith in his God. In the end he saw in his own reflection the face of a leader. He was transformed!

Do you feel that gentle nudge, or perhaps the knock on the door that won't be silenced? Are you looking to others to fill the void, or are you pointing out your weaknesses? *Pick someone else, God. Can't you see I'm still a work in progress?* God isn't looking at your shortcomings or challenges in the same way as you are.

As I studied the story of Moses, I discovered a fascinating possibility. Moses insisted that his greatest disadvantage was that he stuttered. I believed this to be literal until I stumbled across a historical reference from a guy named Stephen, who reported about Moses,

> Pharaoh's daughter found him and raised him as her own son. Moses was taught all the wisdom of the Egyptians, and he became *mighty in both speech and action.*[8]

According to Stephen, Moses was known for his ability to communicate and lead from the time he was a boy. Perhaps what Moses perceived as a speech impediment was an identity problem instead. This is where I feel free to compare myself to Moses. A long time ago I underrated who I was and what I could do. But God saw the real picture. That's why he spoke those words to me that morning: *Stand before me as the woman you are becoming.*

It's why he speaks them to you as well.

What if I fail?

Shortly after writing about a bird's first flight, I sat in my living room and gazed out the front window. The trees were in full bloom. Flowers burst with color. And then I heard a screeching sound. I saw a baby bird flapping its wings, backed against the tire of my car as two cats circled hungrily. I could feel its terror as it opened its tiny beak and cried for help. I leaped out of my chair and threw open the front door. I shouted at the cats, shooing them away as I screamed and swung at them. The baby bird hopped into the tire well.

I lay on my stomach as an oil spill on the driveway soaked my shirt. I coaxed the bird with gentle words. I reached to grasp it, but it pecked at my hand. I finally grasped it, and it pecked my hand wildly with its sharp little beak, drawing blood from my knuckles. I stood, and the bird struggled out of my careful grasp and fell to the ground. It ran right into the path of the cats.

One cat swept in, grabbed the bird, and ran off.

I sat down on the porch. The scene might have been less painful if I hadn't just encouraged you and others to "fly, baby, fly."

"If you fly and you fall, you're doomed?" I said. "Is that the message, God?" I honestly talked to my Lord, and he showed me a different angle to the story. I could see myself rushing to defend the little bird. I could smell the dust in my nostrils and feel the dirt and oil staining my clothes. I saw the bird straining against me, pecking at my hands until they bled. I saw how I refused to give up.

I saw a picture of God and me. How many times had he walked alongside me when I was afraid? How many times had he gone into the dark places of my life as I attempted to find my way? How many times had I pushed him away, desiring to fight my battles my own way, in my own power—and yet he'd never given up on me. I had a choice to accept his outstretched hand.

I also had an option to turn away from his guidance and unconditional love.

Fly, baby, fly. It's still just as true, but there might be times that you fly and fail, or things don't work out the way you think they should. It doesn't mean your flying days are over, but that you need his gentle hand to lift you up and place you back in the wind of destiny. Perhaps you'll soar on your first attempt, but success very rarely is a one-hit wonder. It's a combination of learning what works and what doesn't. It's redefining your destination as you get closer. It's picking yourself up if you mess up and learning from your mistakes. And the reality is, you may do everything right, and things still will not turn out like you thought they would.

> "I often contradict in my own mind what God says about me, or my abilities. I doubt myself so much, and I hate it. But I can do it. I can be who God has called me to be, not just in the future and down the road a few years, but today, tomorrow, and next week. I must remember to quit worrying about the future and whether or not what I'm doing now is going to get me there. I need to focus on what's going on right now."
>
> Sarah Ballard, thirtysomething

Success isn't always defined by results. C.S. Lewis says, "The only real failure in life is the failure to try." As you try your wings—no matter whether you are 18 or 30—you do so with the understanding that you aren't flying solo. God not only holds the flight plan, but he offers guidance. He is your shelter and safety when you feel afraid or unsure. Psalm 61 says, "God, listen to me shout, bend an ear to my prayer. When I'm far from anywhere, down to my last gasp, I call out, 'Guide me up High Rock Mountain!'"

You're not alone

The apostle James encourages us, "If you don't know what you're doing...pray to the Father. He loves to help. You'll get his help, and won't be condescended to when you ask for it." With God's help I began a journey of transformation, and I'm still on that path! My course is corrected as I follow Christ daily. Just when I think I've arrived, I encounter a new opportunity or challenge or season, and the waltz starts all over again. It's a dance that I have come to love.

What about you? I hope you will now consider the construction process in a whole new way. It's not easy. It's not an overnight process. But you're not alone. If you haven't already, I hope you will consider inviting God to be a partner in the process.

The following questions are intended to move this discussion inward. I invite you to take an honest look at your construction process as you answer them.

Describe your identity when you look in the mirror. What does she look like? Is this different from the way God sees you?

I have a hard time seeing beauty, but I know that God finds beauty in His creation.

Are you ready to spread your wings? What does that mean to you personally?

I think I am, but I'm a little scared. I'm not sure what it means just yet.

Share one thing that seems to get in the way as you step into the next phase of construction.

past relationships

Have you ever felt that you failed? Have you invited God into the cleanup stage?

yes; I'm in the cleanup stage right now. apologies are hard to make.

Dear God, thank you for potential growth. Thank you for the thousand questions that aren't answered yet, because that means there are places yet to go, people to meet, and personal and spiritual discoveries ahead. Thank you for walking with me through the construction process, as I become the woman you desire me to be.

I know what I'm doing. I have it all planned out—plans to take care of you, not abandon you, plans to give you the future you hope for. When you call on me, when you come and pray to me, I'll listen.

—FROM JEREMIAH 29

Blog

Making it big...

Current mood: determined

I grew up the epitome of middle class. I had a great family. My parents had high aspirations for me. When I was three they put me in a Montessori school where I learned valuable life lessons such as how to cut bread into three-dimensional shapes. In elementary school I was in the gifted and talented class and labeled as the teacher's pet. I played the violin. After my grandfather died from cancer I planned to attend Harvard and find a cure.

This was my idea of making it big and making a difference. I say these things only because how adults viewed me profoundly affected my development as a child. My parents and others never intended to make me feel this way, but I felt accepted based on what I did.

As a young teenager, a friend invited me to go to church, and my life was deeply changed. I traveled to the inner city of Houston with my church. For three weeks I worked with a team in the fourth ward, a neighborhood controlled by a crack gang. Somewhere between talking to a woman who desperately wanted out of the neighborhood, walking the streets of the Montrose district at three A.M., and hearing a plea for a "dream center" for that area, my life direction changed. I wanted to work with the urban poor and help meet people's physical and spiritual needs as part of God's plan for my life.

During college, I volunteered at Deep Ellum Church in Dallas, Texas. They ministered to the homeless and to the unique needs of Deep Ellum residents. After graduating I applied to work as an urban missionary, but was turned down. I was considered young and inexperienced. I continued to apply until I was accepted.

Jamie Schneider, urban missionary, twentysomething

TWO

Where do I fit?

A WHILE AGO I WATCHED several episodes of the reality show *The Bachelor,* even though I'm totally against the premise of 25 girls vying for a date with one guy! It all began when I got caught up in the drama of a girl named Kristen, one of the beautiful bachelorettes. Kristen was funny and didn't pretend to be anything but herself. One night she was chosen for the one-on-one date, and she and the bachelor met for dinner in Paris. The night held just the perfect ambiance. They dined at the Eiffel tower. There was a sprinkle of starlight above them.

As they dined, a single red rose sat in the middle of the table, a reminder to Kristen that if she didn't measure up, she would be sent home. Perhaps she should have paid attention to the rose, but instead she remained true to herself. Things seemed to go well until she read a poem. The camera zoomed in on the bachelor's patient expression. Then halfway through dinner, Kristen cut an orange peel into a moon shape. She turned away, then turned back around. She had slipped the peel over her teeth and "smiled" at the bachelor with her fake orange-peel teeth. She laughed, inviting her date to join in the silly moment.

He didn't get it.

And she didn't get a rose.

The media flurry afterward suggested that she should have tried harder to fit in. If she had hidden her endearing goofiness, she could have marched past the one-on-one date to a second and third opportunity. But Kristen didn't fake it. She refused to pretend to be something or someone that she was not in order to be accepted. She lived a life of authenticity in front of the bachelor, the camera crew, and the millions of viewers who tuned in each week. She knew exactly who she was, and so did the people around her.

Now that's a prize worth keeping.

When Richard and I got married, he was a country guy and I was a city girl. He graduated with 35 members in his senior class. I graduated with nearly 600. Though I loved living outside the city limits and even owned a horse named Annie, I was still the girl who grew up in a city neighborhood and went to city schools.

One Christmas Richard handed me a large box. I ripped open the paper and exclaimed when I realized it was a very large shoe box. My first thought was, *Boots!* I could imagine the soft feel of leather and how they would look with a certain outfit hanging in the closet. I pushed aside the tissue and took a deep breath when I realized they were...cowboy boots.

There's nothing wrong with cowboy boots; in fact, vintage boots can look pretty cool with the right skirt or jeans. But these were riding boots. Real cowboy boots like the pair that one of my best friends, a world contender in the horse circuit, wears. She looks stunning in them.

But I'm no cowgirl.

I felt awkward, like I was wearing a costume. But I love my husband, so I wore the boots and a pair of cowgirl jeans (my second Christmas gift from my husband) on a date. We ran into friends that night, and my girlfriend pulled me aside. "New look, huh?"

I tried to explain. "Richard really thought they would look nice on me," I sighed.

"Do you like them?"

"Not really." I explained I was trying to be gracious. After all, they were a Christmas present.

"Be true to yourself, Suz," my friend advised. "If it's not you, you're not doing him any favors by pretending."

This story is not about fashion. It's about knowing who we are. It's about forgoing faking it to embrace who we are. Why do women often struggle with trying to find where they fit? Because we are so busy trying to maintain a false image that we fail to discover where we *truly* fit.

Where do I fit? I fit in the arms of a man who loves me for who I am, even when I tactfully let him know I'm a city girl at heart. He loves my laugh. He thinks it is cool that I love to dance with him to '70s music in the living room. I fit in full-time ministry even though my husband is my encourager rather than the lead player in that ministry. His support is a gift, and I return that support wholeheartedly as he pursues what God has placed on his heart. I fit in my friends' lives, even though we are different ages and have different backgrounds and interests. I don't have to try to be something I'm not. I have discovered the power of being real with whoever I'm with, and wherever I may be.

I fit. You fit. We all fit, but finding that place can be the biggest challenge of all.

Live an authentic life

When I began to live honestly in my own skin, no matter how different I was from my friends who were Christians, I felt for the first time in my life that I understood my purpose.
God's plan for my life is so much bigger than my expectations.
ALLISON BOTTKE, FIFTYSOMETHING AUTHOR OF *GOD ALLOWS U-TURNS*

What is your red rose? What is put in front of your nose as

a reminder that you need to fit in? Do you feel that you have to masquerade or play a part to win the job, the guy, the friend—or the favor and acceptance? The reality is, there will always be expectations, even from those who love you best.

Allison Bottke is one of my heroes. She has a warm, sparkly personality. She's open, and she has a laugh that rocks. Like me, she loves vintage jewelry. Allison's road to womanhood was laced with wrong turns. She had a baby before she was ready. She married a physically abusive man, and the marriage disintegrated. She gained a great deal of weight as she struggled with all the complexities, and her life hit bottom when she plunged into addiction.

Years later she became a Christian, and her life slowly bloomed as she found her true self. She discovered that her life was of great value to God. She married a man who loved her fully. She lost over 100 pounds.

Allison is a beautiful woman, but she is stunning not because of her weight loss, but because she is one of the most genuine people I have ever met. I treasure her friendship. Years after her transformation, she wrote a book that spawned a spiritual movement called God Allows U-Turns. Several books later, she believes even more strongly in second chances and in spiritual U-turns.

Nevertheless, she once struggled with people who tried to make her wear ill-fitting pious clothing. "I spent my first 35 years not knowing God. I experienced abuse, addiction, and even abortion. Now that I am a believer, after making a huge U-Turn in my life, I sometimes find I have a somewhat different view of the world than many of my Christian friends. My journey before finding God gave me insight that many of my fellow brothers and sisters in Christ don't have."

For a long time, Allison hid her opinions, feelings, and thoughts because of her previous experiences, thinking she was "less than" or damaged. One day she realized her history could be shared with others. Others who didn't share her past might not understand,

but that was okay! She shed the expectations of others and found new freedom. "When I began to be myself, to transparently share all the garbage that made up so much of my earlier life, I began to make a difference. God made me who I am. I made wrong turns and wrong choices, but I came to a place of faith so that I could tell others that it's never too late to turn toward God. If I tried to fit someone else's image or expectations in order to fit in, I would not be able to share the healing message that God Allows U-Turns. He began to use me when I began to live an honest, authentic life for Him."

> "For a while I thought I had to fit in. In order to arrive as a woman, I thought, I would have to fit in with society's definition of a woman or even what our church says I should be. I guess I thought there was somewhat of a mold of what a Christian wife or woman would be. I don't think that anymore. At this point I am just trying to be myself and I think that is the only way I will arrive as a woman."
>
> MELISSA HALL, TWENTYSOMETHING

Misinformed conformity

Today the pressure to conform is greater than ever before. I worked with teens for nearly two decades, and I watched girls as young as 11 strive to be accepted. The cultural messages are strong, and they are getting stronger. They start early: You are supposed to be a certain size. You should look and sound a certain way. You are seen for your body before your mind or your soul.

Unfortunately, there are also pressures even in the faith world. Nice Christian girls don't laugh too loud. They don't burp. They must look like they just came out of the department store, but be humble enough to pretend that fashion doesn't really matter. They don't hang out with people who don't know God (which always makes me wonder how we're supposed to share our faith). And they don't break the barriers of ministry.

Contrary to popular opinion, the Bible is a textbook on strong women. It shares stories of women who may not have fit a cultural or religious model in their day, but were instrumental in God's plans. In Judges 4 and 5, we find the story of Deborah, a leader and a judge who saved Israel from the Canaanites. In 1 Samuel 25 we find Abigail, a woman who, at great personal risk, made amends for her husband's mistake. In Ezra 2, Nehemiah 7, and Psalm 68 we find female worshipers and musicians.

In the New Testament we find Mary, the mother of Jesus, a woman who bravely carried the Christ child though she faced rejection from her community. We see women disciples like Joanna and Mary, who served with Jesus. We meet Anna, a widow who served as a prophetess in the temple in Jerusalem (Luke 2), and Lydia, a seller of purple fabric, who opened her home to Paul when he was released from jail, in spite of danger to herself. And we find a description of a biblical woman in Proverbs 31. She is a person of integrity. She is an entrepreneur. She is loved and honored by her husband and children.

> "I'm growing. The TV images, the billboard images, the radio images—the worldly images that haunt me everywhere I go—I'll never live up to those. God wants to impress his image on my heart, and that's what will make me a real woman."
>
> B.J. Hamrick, twentysomething

I don't know what these women wore or what their hair looked like. I don't know if they could be pictured as the perfect woman, or if they received criticism for their actions. All I know is that history records their actions, describing them as brave women who lived life fully, leaving a legacy in both the private and public areas of their lives.

In 1 Samuel 16 God gives the prophet Samuel this advice: "Looks aren't everything. Don't be impressed with his looks and stature. I've already eliminated him. God judges persons differently than humans do. Men and women look at the face; God looks into the heart."

If God doesn't judge us by what is on the exterior, then why do we? You fit when you live authentically, from the inside out. Let's talk about three truths that will help as you find your unique place in the world.

1. "Fitting in" is different than accepting that you fit.
2. First accept yourself, and then you'll be able to accept others.
3. Finding a mentor helps you find your way.

Cramming moons into diamond shapes

After Kristen left *The Bachelor,* the media labeled her date as the worst reality-show crash and burn of the century. But out of the limelight she was flooded with e-mails of support (and offers of both friendship and romance) from around the world. When Kristen was asked why her strategy had failed, she informed the media that it hadn't failed. She had remained faithful to her plan. She told one reporter, "My strategy was to be true to myself and true to others."[1]

Who knew that you could find life-changing advice on a reality show?

My friend Allison *fits.* She's a perfect match for the task at hand. She is able to walk into a room and, with warmth and vitality, talk about real stuff. She speaks to people others may never reach. It's her niche!

Do you remember the game you played as a toddler where you fit moons and circles and diamonds into a yellow plastic ball? The problem arose when you tried to cram the moon into the space for the diamond. No matter how much pressure you put on it, it wouldn't go in. Eventually you figured it out: Moons go in the moon shape. Diamonds fit in the diamond shape. Have you tried to fit into a moon shape when God made you a diamond? Take off the mask. Get real with others, but first with yourself. Who are you, really? Do you love comedy, or are you serious? Are you sharp and witty or soft and gentle? Do you love to make your home beautiful, or do you prefer comfort over elegance?

God knows you. He formed you. Your quirks. Your laugh. Your funky or traditional personality. Stop fighting against that, and stop molding yourself or your passions to look like someone else. This isn't permission to shout out to the world, "This is who I am, so deal with it." It's an invitation for you to discover what God wants from *you*, how your unique talents and abilities fit into his plan, and how you can unearth the deeper qualities inside you as you find your place in life. When you try to be something you are not, according to Allison Bottke, "You're telling God that he didn't know what he was doing when he created you. We are unique and special, and God has a plan and purpose for our lives. Trying to be someone we are not is going against a divine plan."

Miss Congeniality vs. Miss Efficient

On a rugged overseas trip a friend called me Miss Congeniality for the first few days. She didn't mean any harm. I genuinely love people and I'm inherently optimistic. I'm a glass-all-the-way-full kind of girl and each person I meet I see as a potential friend. Though the trip, our work, food and lodging were harsh, all I could see was how cool it was. I was eating and sleeping in a boat surrounded by the rain forest, anacondas, and piranha. It doesn't get any more amazing than that! After a few days, my new friend realized that I am joyful by nature (she called it perky; I totally disagree), and she and I became friends. In the past, when I was younger, I would have worried about winning favor from her or other women. I might have even altered my behavior to fit her expectations, or just took a hike and avoided the matter.

But when I learned to accept myself, I was able to accept others much more freely. Just as I wish to be loved for who I am, I must

be willing to understand others. On that trip, it took all of our natural abilities to accomplish our goals. People canoed down a piranha-infested river to find medical and dental assistance. They lined up in each village in the early morning and stood in the heat for hours. My friend was efficient. She dispensed medicine and advice and met physical needs. My role was to pray, to visit, to offer a hug and compassion. We all worked well together, and I came not only to admire my friend, but also to treasure the relationship with this woman as the week progressed.

You and I are a part of something larger. Understanding this keeps our significance from blowing up into self-importance. It keeps the "if onlys" at bay: *If only she could be like the rest of us. If only she didn't dress that way. If only she were nicer/quieter/louder/prettier/plainer/more ambitious/less driven...*Women are notorious for this. Living life as you pound others (or yourself) into a carbon copy is a frustrating existence for everyone. You miss out on the gifts and talents and unique personality of others. You might miss out on a really great friend, even if she's Miss Efficient and you're Miss Congeniality.

Who is your mentor?

You find where you fit as you learn from others. In Amy Tan's novel *Saving Fish from Drowning,* one of the characters climbs a 1000-step stairway to the top of an ancient shrine. He is exhausted, but fakes it. He stops several times as he climbs the steep stairs, pretending that he had it under control, when the truth is he wasn't sure that he'd make it to the top. When he finally arrives at the peak he is bathed in sweat, and yet there are refreshed and relaxed tourists all around him. He discovers that just on the other side of the shrine there was an escalator.

Sure, he made it to the top, but there was an easier way.

At age 47, I have made mistakes and paid the price. I've learned what works and what does not. Some of my efforts produced success. Other insights were earned through painful misjudgments or failures. Some of my most valuable insights came from older women who had walked the road before me. They saw some things that I did not. They knew the potholes on the way to destiny, and were grateful to share. Those insights accelerated my growth.

> "Around my freshman year of college, I developed a close relationship with my youth pastor's wife, Tammy. She was sharp, and quick-witted, and no-nonsense. She prayed with us and for us, and laughed with us, and talked about sex and relationships. Yet for all of her fun and wisdom, she was undeniably a woman...a real woman...not some plastic shell. She was instrumental in drawing me out and encouraging me to let down the walls I had built up to protect myself. It was during this time that I started understanding the value in community, in intimate friendships and relationships, and that I actually did need more than just myself and God to make it through."
>
> Angie Yandell, twentysomething

The mentor relationship

Paul was a church planter during Bible times. He traveled widely and helped establish new churches in areas where the Christian faith was just blossoming. He encouraged pastors through the uncertain waters of leadership.

He was also a mentor. Timothy benefited from Paul's experience. Timothy's dream was to be a leader in a church. Though he came from a good family and was educated, he was also wise enough to invite Paul to serve as his role model. He traveled with Paul. He watched the older man encounter opposition, persecution, and suffer unfair punishments. He listened as Paul taught how to live the Christian faith. He had a front-row seat as his mentor exercised authority in difficult situations and managed complex people.

Later, when Timothy became a leader at a church in Ephesus, his mentor continued to encourage him with letters. Their relationship flourished. But then there was a metamorphosis. A note

arrived from Paul one bleak day. The papyrus scroll was sent from prison, right before Paul's death. It read,

> Keep your eye on what you're doing; accept the hard times along with the good; keep the Message alive; do a thorough job as God's servant. You take over. I'm about to die, my life an offering on God's altar. This is the only race worth running. I've run hard right to the finish, believed all the way. All that's left now is the shouting—God's applause! Depend on it, he's an honest judge. He'll do right not only by me, but by everyone eager for his coming...Get here as fast as you can.[2]

Though Paul continued to encourage Timothy, he also needed him. The young man stepped into a role of pastor and comrade, and encourager. Their relationship had now come full circle.

Where do you find mentors?

You can find mentors within the pages of books. I expand my perspective by reading books by authors from this century, but also of those of groundbreaking theologians of the day. I learn from history and from their life.

But I also learn from women around me. I see them operating in their unique gifts. I see the benefit of their experiences. I take bits and pieces of what I see, leaving behind what does not fit. That helps me discover what I do not want to do, just as much as what I hope to do.

Are you willing to learn from others? As you look for role models, you might begin by asking yourself these questions:

- Do I know someone who has the same passion(s) as I do?
- Are there qualities (confidence, godliness, humility) that I desire and see operating in her actions and behavior?

If you want to be a great mom, connect with women who do it well. If you want to enjoy a healthy relationship with a man, listen to those who are in a healthy relationship. If you want to break away from the past, seek advice from those who are living productive and happy lifestyles in spite of the past. This is where many women get sidetracked. It makes little sense to seek answers for your love life from someone who's not been able to sustain a healthy relationship. Or to listen to those who shoot down dreams because they are bitter, cynical, or have stopped dreaming. Many women sabotage relationships or plans by inviting or listening to damaging advice.

Your part in a mentorship

You look not only at the mentor, but at yourself. Ask yourself these questions also:

- What do I desire from this mentorship?
- Am I teachable?
- Am I willing to give as much as I receive?

Finding a mentor or role model may seem like a difficult process, but it's simply expanding your friendship base to include people who have qualities or traits you admire. Approach a woman as a friend to talk about your shared interests. Most mentor relationships happen naturally. Chances are that more than one mentor-type relationship will develop as you broaden your circle of friends.

A friend once described her journey to growth as being "FAT." "I want to be faithful, accountable, and teachable," she said. The second quality that you bring to a mentor relationship is a teachable spirit.

My friend Michael is in his early 20s and wants to be a pastor to teens. One night he invited me to a meeting where he was the

speaker. Afterward, he caught up with me. "Shoot straight," he said. "Tell me what you thought."

As his friend, I wanted to help but I hesitated because sometimes people say they want advice, when they really don't. Michael asked again, so I asked him to record his next speaking engagement to listen for the "ums" or "ahs" or times that he deviated from the point. I encouraged him on his strengths, but gave him a few suggestions on how to fine-tune his message. Michael immediately put the suggestions into action. I'm not sure if he needed the advice that I gave, but I know that Michael will succeed because he's teachable.

I wish all experiences were as smooth. One day I received a phone call from a woman who wanted to write a book. "Tell me how to get published," she said.

I explained that there was a writers' group in her hometown and the first step would be to connect with other people who share her passion.

"What's next?"

"I want you to go to the library and check out these books," I said. "They will help you to learn how to write a query letter, a proposal, and a solid first chapter. Then you can—"

"Wait a minute," she interrupted. "I don't have time for all of this. Just tell me how to get a book published. I've got a great idea here, and I want my book to hit the shelves in a few months, not a few years."

I ended the phone call with tact, but the reality is that this woman will most likely never publish a book. She wants instant success. If I had a formula to immediate success I would use it myself! There are steps to be taken that will make her a good writer, and perhaps allow her to place her great idea in the hands of people who will publish it. Having been a writer for a few years, I realize that her aggressiveness—without the benefit of knowledge or experience—will turn an editor away within seconds.

I could have taught her that. I could have helped her eliminate the discomfort zone that she will experience if she takes her book directly to a publisher with that attitude, but unfortunately she will learn it on her own.

Receive, give, and pass it on

A mentor relationship is give and take. Offer to assist on occasion. Pray for the person you're mentoring. Encourage her. As time passes, the relationship will mature. This is the cool part, and the secret that I waited to share until last. Somewhere along the discovery process, you metamorphose. You become an adviser. You become an encourager or teacher.

Look behind you. Not far away is a young woman—perhaps a young girl—trying to find her way, wondering where she fits. You get the opportunity to take what you've learned and share it with others.

Do you ever try to fit in? Why or why not? What is the difference between fitting in and finding a place where you fit?

____

____

Do you respect the differences of other women? Have you ever stopped to think that God might have created them that way? How does that change your thinking?

____

____

In one sentence, describe your passion.

____

____

____

Do you try to fit someone else's standards? How has that kept you from realizing your dreams? Is it really biblical? If so, are you willing to talk about it with God to find what he desires?

Who has been a mentor (formal or informal) for you? What was it about this person that caused him or her to have a positive impact on you?

If you do not have a mentor, brainstorm and list five possibilities. Pray about it. Observe them from a distance. When the time is right, ask one person if she would be interested in mentoring you.

God, I fit! You made me unique. Help me to view myself the way you do rather than try to fit in an image or vocation that fits like a bad suit. Help me to be accepting of my friends and family who are different than me. Bring people into my life who will be truthful and encouraging. Give me a teachable spirit. As I learn, may I become an encourager to others.

Then [Samuel] asked Jesse, "Is this it?
Are there no more sons?" "Well, yes, there's the runt.
But he's out tending the sheep." Samuel ordered Jesse,
"Go get him. We're not moving from this spot until he's
here." Jesse sent for him. He was brought in, the very
picture of health—bright-eyed, good-looking. GOD
said, "Up on your feet! Anoint him! This is the one."
Samuel took his flask of oil and anointed him, with his
brothers standing around watching.
The Spirit of GOD *entered David like a rush of wind,*
God vitally empowering him for the rest of his life.

FROM 1 SAMUEL 16

Blog

My body/my self...

Current mood: grateful

I was a teen when I started talking about my faith with others. Every day one summer I told kids about God, and that he loved them. Every day we memorized scriptures about his love. And every day when I was finished, I ran to the bathroom and threw up. It wasn't the thought of his love that made me sick. It was the physical condition that was slowly eating away at my body. A chronic illness I'd suffered with for four years was wrecking my immune system. At the age of 14, I was five-foot-three and weighed 88 pounds. My bones protruded through my skin, and people noticed. The kids didn't seem to mind. The adults were the cruel ones. Nicknames, inconsiderate comments, and accusations of eating disorders flew from their mouths.

People who didn't know me didn't hesitate to judge me. It wasn't long before I started to hear a little thought in the back of my mind that said, *God can't love someone who looks like you do.* And it wasn't long before I started to believe that thought.

I'm 23 years old now. My body is healed, but sometimes the "God can't love you" thought still haunts me. Sometimes I still feel like that frail 14-year-old girl, desperately alone. Sometimes I feel like God loves everyone except me. Sometimes I feel like I'll never fit in. How can I get past that feeling? How can this almost-college-graduate come to understand the truth that the God of the Universe cares less about how she looks, and more about her heart? How can the woman who has told countless kids about the love of God come to know that love for herself?

B.J. Hamrick, twentysomething

THREE

That little thing called body image

I STOOD IN FRONT OF THE MIRROR. The person frowning back at me in the mirror was lean and long-limbed, except for her stomach. It looked like a cantaloupe (or a small watermelon) as she pooched it out. "Look," I said to my daughter Melissa. "I'm pregnant." She laughed and then pulled a straight face.

I knew that face. I was in trouble. I sucked my stomach back in.

"You know, Mom, that's not a good thing to do."

"What do you mean?" I asked. "I'm just teasing."

"No, you're not, and when you say things like that it affects me," Melissa said. "You should know that. Stop it."

Melissa is petite and gorgeous with blond hair and green eyes. When I walk with her in the mall, heads turn in her direction. *How could my jokes bother her?* She went on to explain. "Sometimes I find myself doing the same thing. Guess where I got it from?"

Ouch.

For the next several days I caught myself saying negative things about my body. I was frustrated when certain types of shirts showed my extra pounds around the middle. I complained to my husband when my jeans fit everywhere but around my stomach or when I had to grab a jacket to cover. Melissa's observation made me realize I was paying a lot more attention to my physical body than I should. Worse, I was modeling this behavior in front of others. The truth is that I am healthy and I'm not overweight. I'm just not the skin-n-bones I once was. I have given birth to three beautiful children, and my body will never be perfect, but that's okay. I'm God's girl. I'm beautifully made in his image. That's a fact etched on my heart and my mind.

Now if only if someone would remind my mouth.

I was a cute baby, but by the time I turned 13 I looked like a rubber band that had stretched overnight. I was all arms and legs with a few sprinkles of freckles across my nose. That was the year my enemy hit with vengeance—psoriasis. My arms and legs were covered in large, pink, scaly sores, and I rubbed stinky tar ointment on my skin every night and wrapped my arms and legs in plastic wrap. My older sister hated sleeping with me because I made crinkly noises all night. I wore long sleeves and long pants even in the summer. I brushed my long brunette hair often to get rid of the flakes. I avoided the school swimming pool like a leper because the other girls would stare at the lesions on my arms and legs. When I hit my 20s a drug company created a new medicine for psoriasis, and the skin disease became manageable.

No more *skritch-skritch* of plastic wrap all night long.

But I still had body-image issues. I was 20 pounds *under*-weight. I wasn't *that* girl—you know, the one that stopped the construction crew in their tracks as they let out long, low wolf whistles. If I sashayed by, they just kept on hammering. I was the woman the lunch person always felt needed an extra helping of mashed potatoes. But the people that mattered most to me accepted me, and their love and friendship was based on things that had nothing to do with weight.

But then, at 31, body image slammed home in an entirely different way. I found a small, hard lump nested on the upper part of my right breast. I was at kids' camp as a counselor, sleeping on a mattress that wrapped around me like a hot-dog bun. The wire frame beneath poked through. As I tossed and turned on the bed of torture, I felt the lump roll just under my flesh. I waited nearly three months for my annual gynecological exam to see what was wrong (bad idea!).

That day my doctor pressed on my breast like a grandma kneading dough. The nurse, a friend of mine, wore a mask of compassion. Something small stirred inside me—fear. But I reasoned with myself one more time: I came for a Pap smear. That was on the other end, so this little lump couldn't be a problem.

Wrong again.

Two days later I was wheeled through cold, hard steel doors for major surgery. I lost a section of my breast. The cancer had spread to my lymph nodes. I started chemotherapy one month later and had a weird reaction, gaining 27 pounds in the first few weeks. After 32 years of trying to gain weight, now my clothes didn't fit. I was fatigued. I didn't know if it was the extra weight or the fact that doctors were blasting cells with toxic chemicals.

The type of cancer that I had was estrogen-positive, so I had a hysterectomy after my radiation and chemo were complete. I woke up that afternoon after surgery and it was 6000 degrees in the room. I was experiencing my first hot flash. I went through menopause before my mom did. I gained weight as my metabolism slowed down like a semi driver hitting the brakes.

My body changed in a hundred different ways because of cancer. The segmented mastectomy left me with one malformed breast. My skin was rough and red due to the radiation. I had several permanent blue tattoo dots on my chest. I alternated between hot and cold, so I slapped sheets on and off throughout the night. I leapfrogged from skinny to not-as-skinny when I gained 35 pounds in less than four months.

I did what I could. I walked every day. I rubbed lotion into my burned and dry skin. I ate foods that nurtured my body, but it took nearly a year to lose 15 pounds. I ate every word I'd ever uttered about "If people really wanted to lose weight, they could."

Ten years later I celebrated a milestone. I turned 42. Ten years! My body had changed, but I was alive, and there was a bonus. The 15 extra pounds that I kept as a souvenir finally gave me a valid reason for buying a bra!

Today I am officially middle-aged—if I live to be 94. There are more changes ahead. I see a white hair cropping up here and there. Laugh lines are creeping around my eyes. Pounds are trying to creep around my waist. But my conversation with Melissa was a reminder that I needed to once again redefine real beauty.

But Suzie, you're ancient. What does this have to do with me?

I had somehow bought into the cultural messages of what is beautiful and what is not, and that's a growing phenomenon, affecting woman of all ages but especially beautiful young women just like you. It shifts the focus from things that matter to things that often do not. For me, I had forgotten that I'm healthy, whole—and yes, I'm beautiful to my children, to my husband, to my friends, and to my God.

God, thank you for true beauty.

You're more than your body

> *Scientists have concluded that there must be something more to us than our brains and our bodies. The Bible makes the same point: Whether it describes you with the words "soul," "spirit," or "heart," the meaning is the same—the real you, the deepest truest you is not your body. You are a living soul.*
>
> LAEL ARRINGTON, FIFTYSOMETHING AUTHOR, RADIO HOST, AND FORMER BEAUTY QUEEN

More than any other generation, this one struggles with body image. Eating disorders have doubled in the last 30 years. The number of healthy, attractive young women dieting and worrying about their weight continues to rise. The age factor is dropping as girls as young as five years old worry about their weight. Approximately five million people are estimated to have eating disorders (anorexia nervosa, bulimia nervosa, binge eating disorder, and other eating problems).[1] In a society that equates beauty with brand names, stick-thin models, and unrealistic expectations, how can you redefine authentic beauty?

> "I am someone who is always working on knowing my faults through and through...but who also knows my strengths through and through. I want to be so aware of my faults that I am not ashamed of them and so confident in my strengths that they are used to the fullest."
>
> Melissa Hall, twentysomething

1. Stop trying to fit unrealistic images.
2. Stay out of the shallow pool.
3. Shift the focus.

Pressure toward unrealistic images

Body image issues can come from many sources, but the overriding demand is to conform to someone else's idea of body image. Angelina Jolie was once quoted as saying, "People have really odd opinions. They tell me I'm skinny, as if that's supposed to make me happy. I feel better when I have more weight on me. So it's when I'm not feeling like myself that people are telling me I look great. It's so strange. No matter what, somehow it's like I'm not enough."[2] If one of the most exquisite women in the world deals with these feelings, is there hope for anyone else?

Pressure can come from family members, especially if they are one body type and you are another. It can come from caustic remarks from well-meaning friends or acquaintances (or perhaps, not so well-meaning), or those who are "just joking." It may have started early when people accepted you based upon your appearance; instead of being you, you were the girl with the great body, or the high school homecoming queen, or the girl everybody wanted to be, which is problematic when your body changes and suddenly you're trying to figure out who you really are underneath.

> "Sometimes I still struggle with this. I compare myself to others. Why do I do this? I know that God has designed me with greatness! And yet I still fall into the trap."
>
> Tiffany Hammonds, twentysomething

Peer pressure is stereotyped as a middle-school obstacle, but many women of all ages struggle with judgment if they don't fit a cultural physical image. The ideal body is promoted as thin—seriously, scarily thin. Beautiful models glide down runways with angular bodies and high cheekbones. Airbrushed celebrities grace the covers of magazines and billboards. Models with Barbie-like figures promote products from deodorant to automobiles to tampons. Girls and women look at these images and wonder why they don't measure up, forgetting that we can't be Barbie because she's not real. She's a fantasy image. Recently a handful of companies, including the one that manufactures Dove, decided to bravely bust stereotypes and to promote women with real bodies. Instead of size 0, the models were size 2 to size 16. Why did they do this? Perhaps it is because the pursuit of a fantasy body leads to unhealthy dieting, binging, or eating disorders. In extreme cases, it can lead to multiple surgeries, distorted mental images of your body or appearance, or a fixation on body parts instead of the whole person.

There are a thousand more important elements to a woman's life! First Corinthians 6 reminds us that our bodies are a gift:

> Didn't you realize that your body is a sacred place, the

> place of the Holy Spirit? Don't you see that you can't live however you please, squandering what God paid such a high price for? The physical part of you is not some piece of property belonging to the spiritual part of you.

Taking care of your body is important. Eating healthy makes sense. But there is a balance. Michelle Graham in *Wanting to Be Her,* writes, "Think of a continuum between two extremes: body obsession and body neglect. A balanced response avoids both extremes."[3] A balanced response allows you to replace the messages that say, "You have to look like this," with the healthier message that says, "Take care of your body," or the spiritual message that says, "Your body is a temple where the Spirit of God lives, so take care of it"[4]—which allows you to pursue deeper personal activities, and to center your attention on who you are separate from your physical appearance.

Swimming in the shallow pool

Sex and the City is wildly popular now in reruns. The show centers on four women in pursuit of fashion and the perfect body, as well as their sex lives. Four friends shop and sleep their way to fabulousness, reflecting the ultimate shallow pool. The message is that the right purse or pair of designer shoes, or a wild romp in bed, will make life worth living. I love shoes. I like a great purse. I like sex with my hubby. But I am frustrated by the implication that as long as you carry a designer bag or wear Prada shoes, or are sexually oversaturated, life is good. That is only one of a hundred different unrealistic messages in these types of programs, and yet women tune in by the millions. Sometimes we are our own worst enemies—fighting against the unrealistic images, but setting the video recorder so we can savor them.

True beauty is found in the loveliness and grace found in laugh lines and eyes that reflect wisdom. It is a body changed by stretch marks due to the birth of a little human being. It's the laugh of a happy woman. It is confidence that comes from the inside out. It's the security that comes from knowing who you are. These types of beauty might not be found on an advertisement, but are lasting and a great deal more satisfying.

Extreme makeover

I believe that every woman is beautiful. I love makeover shows (that don't require surgery)! I think it's fun to find that the right outfit can make you look your best, or having fun with makeup can bring out your smile or the shade of your eyes or skin. I love new hairstyles and cool clothes. But before I have my makeover, I first desire a make*under.* I want God to change me from the inside out. In Galatians 5, we learn what to take off:

> It is obvious what kind of life develops out of trying to get your own way all the time: repetitive, loveless, cheap sex; a stinking accumulation of mental and emotional garbage; frenzied and joyless grabs for happiness; trinket gods; magic-show religion; paranoid loneliness; cutthroat competition; all-consuming-yet-never-satisfied wants; a brutal temper; an impotence to love or be loved; divided homes and divided lives; small-minded and lopsided pursuits...

But if you take these off, won't you be left naked, vulnerable? God doesn't leave you without a new wardrobe. In the next verses, we find some nice new "under" wear to put on. Things like love, joy, peace, patience, kindness, goodness, faithfulness, gentleness, and self-control. The truth is, we aren't always thoughtful. We don't always do the right thing in every instance. Sometimes you want to give in to your emotions and let the pieces fall where they land. But real beauty takes root when you go beneath the exterior and allow the Holy Spirit to give you lasting beauty.

Changing your focus

Lael Arrington was voted "Most Beautiful" in her high school.

She was first runner-up for Miss Teenage Houston. Today, she is in her 50s and suffers from debilitating rheumatoid arthritis. She has undergone several surgeries to replace or repair affected joints.

My friend Lael is gorgeous. She has not allowed arthritis to rob her of a full life. She is an author and the host of a radio program called *The Things That Matter Most.* She says this about her changing body image:

> Our bodies are like a paint brush. Picture the brush extending from the middle of a closed stage curtain, poised to paint a picture on an empty canvas. For 25 years I have battled rheumatoid arthritis. I think my brush has become more of a sketch pencil. Yet there is hope. The deepest truest me will one day toss this sketch pencil aside. I will enjoy the beauty of my soul reflected in my new body. A beauty only made possible by picking up that chalk and, by God's grace, drawing another picture, another day.[5]

Your body will change

Your exterior will change. You can delay it. You can buy great clothes and go to the best beauticians. You can use botox or you can add inches to your bustline. I'm not saying that these are wrong, but if they become an obsession—and they often do—aren't we missing the point? What might women discover if we went deeper? What spiritual beauty lies within you and me? When this takes place, you find the real you. Lael affirms this. "We ultimately do not control our bodies. God does. And he wants to give you real beauty—the beauty of your heart. Your soul. As we grow in Christ, age, and lose control of our body, we can gain the beauty of a soul that sees and delights in all that God is and has for us for eternity."

Recently I sat with a young woman in her 20s. She's a size zero. She's tiny and stunning. She's also consumed with her appearance.

In her mind, she is too big in some areas. Her face isn't as perfect as it should be. She meticulously analyzes her features, wishing that this or that were different. She spends a great deal of time thinking about her appearance. On the outside, you would never see her personal battle. She's intelligent. She's fun to hang out with. She's one of those twenty-somethings that appear to have it all.

> "I'm determined that I am not going to pick on myself today. I'm going to focus on what I CAN do. I can love on the 4-year-olds where I work and show them God's love because they certainly don't care what I look like. They only care if I love and accept THEM the way they are. And I can love on my own kids and my husband and be honest that I'm not perfect but I can love them with perfect love. Yeah, that's what I'm gonna do."
>
> SARAH BALLARD, THIRTYSOMETHING

As we talked, I suggested that this might be deeper. I asked her to consider that it might be a spiritual battle.

I asked her to refocus, and to consider that we all have vulnerable areas where our spiritual adversary can and will use to distract us from what really matters. Hebrews 12 suggests we are in a race.

> Do you see what this means—all these pioneers who blazed the way, all these veterans cheering us on? It means we'd better get on with it. Strip down, start running—and never quit! No extra spiritual fat, no parasitic sins.

My friend was so engrossed in her looks that it had become obsessive and unhealthy. It was tripping her up in her race, distracting her from who she was, and where God was trying to take her. In the book *Mind Games*, Matthew Paul Turner shares the story of his friend Cheryl. She felt so ugly that she became obsessed with her appearance, much like my friend. He describes the lies whispered to Cheryl as a cage, and how she battled to climb out of that cage so that she could think about something besides her body image. He says,

> She found out the hard way something that we all must understand: Our minds hold a great deal of power over our lives. The objective truth—God's truth—is that Cheryl is valuable to God (he created her!) and thus she is infinitely worthy. Her place in the kingdom of God is not based on superficial qualifications. God looks at the heart, not the skin. Cheryl's value to God is a truth she could build her life around.[6]

Do you ever obsess about your looks? Do you have a bad day if you don't look the way that you want? What might happen if women pursued wisdom, knowledge, compassion, joy, and service to others as doggedly as physical perfection? Christine Hassler, in *20-Something, 20-Everything,* believes that we will find something much greater, suggesting that "the energy we direct toward these standards, and the importance we place upon them, delay discovery of who we really are."[7]

Who are you really? Have fun with clothes, makeup, and fashion, but don't let them or someone else's definition of beauty rob you of discovering who you are.

I own a 12X-magnifying mirror. In my 12X mirror my flaws are larger than life. If I stare long enough, I lose sight of the bigger picture. I only see a distorted image. Our mirror is Christ. He goes beneath the surface to show us our heart. Why don't you take a minute and invite him to join you as you examine your thoughts about a little thing called body image.

Do you ever obsess with one or more physical characteristics of your body or face? Name the characteristic and one recent incident.

____

____

How does that affect you (or others around you)?

Do you believe that there are unreal expectations placed on women your age? Have you bought into those unrealistic expectations? Why?

You might not be able to change culture, but you can change you. Name one inner quality you'd like to nurture. What is one way to do that?

You are valuable to God. What might happen if you changed "mirrors" to see yourself through that spiritual truth vs. cultural expectations?

Name the things that you believe will be important to you 10 years from now, 20 years from now, and 50 years. Are you willing to shift your focus to these characteristics or goals?

Dear God, I am made in your image. I matter to you. Please make me wise. Let me be grateful for physical health. Thank you that I can live a strong and healthy life, but thank you also for inner beauty. Will you join me as I pursue joy, wisdom, peace, and selflessness? I want to look like you.

If you're serious about living this new resurrection life with Christ, act *like it. Pursue the things over which Christ presides. Don't shuffle along, eyes to the ground, absorbed with the things right in front of you. Look up, and be alert to what is going on around Christ—that's where the action is. See things from* his *perspective. Your old life is dead. Your new life, which is your* real *life—even though invisible to spectators—is with Christ in God.* He *is your life. When Christ (your real life, remember) shows up again on this earth, you'll show up, too—the real you, the glorious you.*

FROM COLOSSIANS 3

PART TWO: RELATIONSHIPS

Building your community

Everything we know about God's Word is summed up in a single sentence: Love others as you love yourself. That's an act of true freedom.

FROM GALATIANS 5

Blog

Still learning...

Current mood: serious

I have this soapbox and theories for dating and marriage, but I'm still trying to figure out what it means and looks like. I have friends who don't want to be single, but they refuse to put out any vibes or show interest or initiate conversation because they've been conditioned with some weird theology that only a male can initiate such things. I have another friend who has been in a long-term relationship, but they've never had the all-important "DTR" (define the relationship) talk. In my relationship, I've realized that God made us the way we are for a reason. I am confident, independent, and opinionated. I've found someone who can put up with all of that. Not just put up with it, but complement it.

I'm learning. I have found that the essence of the word *submit* is service, motivated by love. We love each other. So we serve each other. We consider the other more important than ourselves, and we show our love and service by doing for the other. It is give and take. It's why I have missed sleeping in all fall long to enjoy "college game day" on ESPN and to watch football from Saturday morning to Monday night. But it's also why he has given up the Miami game to take me to the *Lion King,* and why he misses the Sunday night games to watch *The Amazing Race* with my sister and brother-in-law, and why he's missed other things to go with me to the mall while I hunt for a pair of pants that minimize love handles while maximizing the nonexistent booty I have. We give up our preferences from time to time in order to serve.

Angie Yandell, twentysomething

FOUR

Love, marriage, and great sex

I SAT IN MY MUSTANG. My friend Michelle drove while I sat in the passenger window and whistled at a car. It was my first week of college. I felt free. Until the white car I'd whistled at made a U-turn and pulled behind us. Suddenly my normally shy self felt incredibly foolish. I slipped out of the window and into the passenger seat.

"What are we going to do?" I asked.

My friend pulled over. So did they. Two college guys stepped out. The driver was medium height, dark-skinned...with a smile that gripped my heart.

Richard says he fell in love with me that day, seeing my hair fly in the wind, my smile open and carefree. All I know is that I should have been sitting in the car with my seatbelt firmly buckled. Of course, that's how I see things now—as a mom of three children who I hope will never ride in the window of their car, or whistle at guys they don't know.

But that night began the adventure of a lifetime. Today, 27 years later, I'm married to the guy with the smile. He's not the man who fixes my car, or the person who takes out the trash. I'm not the house cleaner, or the woman who serves up a tasty dish of roast. Do we do all these things together? Yes, but those are tasks.

Our love? That's a whole different story. He's still the guy I fell in love with on a calm summer day, and I'm still the woman who captured his heart.

The day after I met him, Richard stood outside my college dorm window, a lazy smile across his face. "Come help me," he said, holding up a Santa-sized duffel bag full of laundry.

I didn't know his last name. I didn't know the name of his hometown. All I knew is that he was connected to that smile. There was love in the air. There had to be, because I wasn't looking to do laundry on any day—much less that beautiful September morning. But I found myself trekking over to a laundromat, where Richard started piling clothes in the washer. "Wait a minute," I said, hopping down from the washer where I sat Indian-style. "Reds and whites don't mix. Surely you know that."

He was a quick student and sorted his jeans and T-shirts separate. I noticed that as he pulled clothes from the bag, they seemed extremely clean. A few items appeared to be folded. *Was he a neat freak? Did he fold his dirty clothes?* We sat in the laundry room for the next three hours with the swish of water and the hum of dryers as our background music. He was sweet, funny, and he listened as I told him my life story—at least the good parts. He told me about his large extended family. I sketched in a verbal picture of my siblings, mom, and dad.

He was raised on a farm. I was raised in the city. We had many differences, but there was a definite connection. He was a Christian and talked openly about his faith. He was outgoing and I loved his easy confidence. Afterwards we drove to the lake with my friends. Richard took me by the hand and gently pulled me to the shoreline where we sat and chatted longer. Then he leaned over and kissed me. I didn't expect it; it was gentle and sweet.

A few years later Richard and I were with friends, and I told them how I fell for him during an afternoon at the laundromat.

Richard laughed and pulled me close. "Did I never tell you?" he asked.

"Tell me what?"

"I wanted to get to know you without all of your friends around so I decided to throw all my clothes in a bag and hoped that you'd take pity on me. They were all clean. Every last piece."

"Did you know how to do laundry?" I asked.

"I could have figured it out."

It wasn't the smoothest move ever made, but it worked and I'm grateful. We've washed hundreds of loads of clothes together since that time.

And I still love his kisses.

Looking for love

> *The more passion we express toward God, the more passion God then boomerangs back to us for our love life. What a gift!*
>
> Pam Farrel, fortysomething author and speaker

So much has changed in the past few years, but especially in the area of relationships. The playing field appears to be much larger with global connections through Facebook, MySpace, and online journals such as Xanga. It is not unusual to share your deeper thoughts with 500 of your friends. But sharing the *real* you in person can be difficult. In spite of online and everyday acquaintances, you might wonder if the guy you hope to meet exists. Perhaps you feel cynical or frustrated because the meaning of love has been diluted in this culture, or you've been hurt by someone you loved—someone who was supposed to be a good person, but turned out to be a poor choice. So you wait, or worse, you don't wait, while you try to sort out real love from the convoluted and confusing societal messages. Most of the twentysomething women I meet don't want a casual hookup, though many have fallen for that trap. Others wait, but aren't sure where to begin. *Is it okay to make the first move if I meet a great guy? What do I do if I live in a guy-wasteland and there's no one to choose from?*

> "I want someone who is trustworthy most of all, a best friend to laugh with, cry with and share my whole life with, someone to love me selflessly and loves my girls as well."
>
> MEGAN MUSTAIN, TWENTYSOMETHING

Many express a longing for intimacy, desiring a man who can see beyond the exterior and relate to the woman inside. Some look at the love of their grandparents, and wonder if this kind of love still exists.

The issue of dating, guys, sex, and marriage was the most intense conversation I had with my twentysomething friends. Many of the questions were the same, whether the person was single, in an exclusive relationship, or married. One married twentysomething couple recently shared this heartfelt plea with Richard and me: We don't know how to do this! Our parents weren't able to stay married. Is it foolish to think that we can do it when no one has showed us how?

Let's talk about some of the questions posed in these conversations:

1. Is there such a thing as real love?
2. Is it possible to be monogamous?
3. What do I do if I'm already in a bad relationship?
4. What does a good marriage look like?

Love is more than a warm body

Casual hookups aren't love. In fact, real love is much deeper than sex—casual or committed. It's more of an attitude of one person toward another. Paul described love in 1 Corinthians 13:

Love never gives up.
Love cares more for others than for self.
Love doesn't want what it doesn't have.
Love doesn't strut,
Doesn't have a swelled head,
Doesn't force itself on others,
Isn't always "me first,"
Doesn't fly off the handle,
Doesn't keep score of the sins of others,
Doesn't revel when others grovel,
Takes pleasure in the flowering of truth,
Puts up with anything,
Trusts God always,
Always looks for the best,
Never looks back,
But keeps going to the end.

Many times women want love and a relationship. They want to know that someone finds them attractive. But things go wrong when a woman wants it so much that they accept a relationship that hooks a "we" over their name instead of a nurturing relationship based on the characteristics found in 1 Corinthians 13. Why accept a man who is not loving, who is not kind, who forces himself and his faults on others? In those relationships, love = a warm body. A couple is created, but the elements required for lasting love are lacking. I'm distressed when I see girls and twentysomethings accept far less than they should. Recently I spoke at a school and one young woman said, "I know I have a good day when a guy talks to me."

What?

I understand what it is to love people and then to lose them.

I know what it is to be acutely lonely. Because I have experienced these, I require more in my relationships, not just with my husband, but with those who are in the intimate circle of my life. It is something I also desire to give to them. You are worthy to be loved. You have love to give. Relationships won't be perfect, because we are all far from perfect. But if someone is looking to find a quick connection, someone to play with, or to toss aside, you're not their girl, and never should be.

Let's do a 180

Then there is the other opposite attitude. Standards are so stringent that the perfect man never arrives, or if he does he can't live up to them, so he's booted out until the next *perfect* guy comes around the corner. What does he look like? Perhaps he's financially sound but not money-hungry, dresses nice but not into clothes more than you, sensitive yet manly, romantic but rugged. He needs to look nice, smell great, and—because it's important—he needs to be someone who lives out his faith. It's difficult to find someone who embodies all of these characteristics because the person who is "perfect" rarely is. What if God's guy for you is kind and sensitive, but skinny—or a man of faith, but not the rugged man of your dreams?

The reality is that most people grow into your perception of them. When I first met Richard, I was thin and awkward, and yet as the years passed I grew into his love for me. It was so big and so encouraging that after time I saw myself through his eyes. For many years Richard greeted me in the morning with these words: "You're beautiful, baby." The truth is, I'm far from lovely in the early morning hours. I wake up with hair mashed on one side of my head, and rising with static on the other. My breath is funky until I apply some Crest. I don't wake up singing or sweet-natured. I'm more like a zombie for the first few minutes. For a long time when Richard would utter those words, I would grin

and retort, "You're such a liar." And then one day I stopped saying that. Somehow over the years I began to see myself through his eyes. My husband found me beautiful even with my obvious flaws, and that was a truth I could live with.

Your list might read: tall, hot, loves rock but not afraid to listen to some cool jazz, wears funky clothes, drives a hybrid Honda (because he cares about the environment), fair but not freckled. What happens when the really cool guy who is short, kinda cute, loves jazz, drives a Dodge Durango with a hemi engine, and is dark-haired with beautiful dark skin, comes into the picture? Set standards in your relationships, but leave room for the man God has for you.

Now he's hot—now he's not

Look beneath the exterior when setting standards. A man may have all the outer glamour, but it's the interior that counts in real love. The exterior will change over the course of 20, 30, and 40 years of marriage anyway. Your definition of "hot" will change. Remember my husband's curly brown hair? Gone! But he's still smoking hot. The outside will alter due to age, but the inside of a man deepens. If his character is shallow, unless there is a significant life change, then that shallowness becomes a river of insensitivity. If a man is kind and attentive, there's a great chance he will become the catch of the century once someone sees his potential. These are questions you can ask when looking at Mr. Right (or Mr. Wrong):

- Is he honest? Or is integrity unimportant to him?
- Is he kind to others? Or does he play with people's hearts?
- Is he a 1 Corinthians 13 man?
- Will I be happy waking up with this person 25 years from now when his physique has changed and all I have left is what is on the inside?

Choosing a man who has depth is vital, for love is tested throughout a relationship. It needs depth to hold fast as you learn to trust each other. It needs character as you blend your dreams and different beliefs, family traditions, and practices into one. When you marry, you walk into someone else's family, and perhaps a new city. You merge your home. There are a thousand different things that seemed small before you lived with each other that seem huge now. I remember the first time I walked into a dark bathroom in the middle of the night and fell into the toilet because my husband had left the seat up. Before we were married, it was his house and his toilet. Now that we shared a house, he needed to change his habit. Falling into the toilet in the middle of the night—ewww!

Finances peck at your commitment to love each other. Children arrive, which is both amazing and complex. You reach for him and find a little one with a wet diaper lying in that special place once reserved just for you and your guy. Real love matures as you commit to work hard and choose to live unselfishly with another human being. Some think that attraction to each other is enough, and it's not and never will be. Real love is selfless love that will take you through both of those extremes, and yet remain consistent. It's hard work, and that's why choosing the right guy is something you decide long before your "he's so hot" switch flips on.

Red-hot monogamy

Pam Farrel is one of the most fun and compassionate woman I've met. She's also the author of *Red-Hot Monogamy*. She and her husband, Bill, host marriage retreats across the country. This past year they were filming a video to go with one of their relationship books. When the cameras cut away, she and her husband of 27 years stood alone on the shoreline. There were no lights, no lectures. It was simply a man and a woman standing alone, still in love years after the "I do."

What is the key to their success? Pam and Bill decided early in their relationship to make choices that would help their marriage last. "One choice was to be other-centered in our relationship," says Pam. To be other centered means you make two lists. Not just an inventory of qualities for the man you hope to meet, but also a list for yourself, asking,

- What will/do I bring to a relationship?
- What qualities can I work on to be the woman/wife/ person I long to be?
- Am I willing to work hard to have a healthy relationship?

If you are an other-centered woman, you encourage rather than point out faults. You practice patience. You pray for your boyfriend or spouse. You focus on interior qualities like integrity and goodness. Whether you are married or currently in a relationship, you work together to create an other-centered relationship.

I continue to work on this in my relationship with Richard. There are things that I can do that make him happy, and there are simple things that bring me joy. He opens the door for me. He checks on spooky noises in the middle of the night. I touch him—it's definitely one of his strongest love languages. He loves for me to stay in his arms, rather than pat his back and pull away. There are times that I fall short, and so does he, because real love isn't a fairy tale. But we know that our relationship will last because it's a safe, loving, selfless place to be.

Really great sex

For all the sexual saturation in our society, fewer and fewer people seem to find fulfillment. Perhaps this is why the boundaries continue to spiral deeper and relationships move farther away from monogamy. I've only made love to one man, and according to some, I'm missing out on something. I read an excerpt from a CNN transcript where Bill Maher, host of *Politically Incorrect,* talks with Larry King. The host asks Maher if his relationships are monogamous, and this was his response:

> MAHER: Well, monogamy, Larry: That's the "m" word...you know, that's one of the lies that you have to perpetrate to be married.
>
> KING: You think you can't be monogamous?
>
> MAHER: Oh, I think you can be. I think it's a lie to say you're enjoying it.[1]

I believe monogamous sex is the most enjoyable sex of all. It is waking up in the arms of someone who deeply cares for you the next day. My friend Pam Farrel describes monogamy in a different light: "Orgasm over and over, year after year, in a committed, loving, marital relationship of trust and admiration—wow—that's worth it!"

Great sex is more than intercourse. After nearly 20 years of ministry, I've seen behind the scenes and into the lives of many young women. Casual sex leaves a woman feeling empty. The more partners—the longer a woman opens her life to multiple men who may or may not care about her as a person—the more meaningless it all seems after a while. Sex is sharing sensual and physical passion with your mate founded on attraction, deep love, and nurturing each other. It is also a spiritual act. First Corinthians 6 says, "There's more to sex than mere skin on skin. Sex is as much spiritual mystery as physical fact. As written in Scripture, 'The two become one.'"

Good sex leaves you feeling better, rather than worse, when the act is completed. It's waking up with that person the next morning, and the next, and 20 years later. Does it take work to keep sex fresh and alive in a marriage? Absolutely. When I first met Jill Savage, it was shortly after I read her great book *Is There Sex After Kids?* I was surprised to read that Jill and her husband,

Mark, set aside a day and time to be intimate with each other. I felt a little sheepish knowing what occurred in the Savage household, but encouraged that this couple considered intimacy with each other as a priority. Mark and Jill have been married for over a quarter of a century and have five children. They are partners in ministry and in life. When they close the door, they've made arrangements to have time alone. There is no guessing or "what if's," but a sense of anticipation throughout the day. It doesn't mean that a couple doesn't have impulsive moments with each other or that sex is limited to a certain number of opportunities. Rather, it's creating an attitude that says "we matter."

> "We both have a deep respect for each other and for each of our decisions to wait until we are married to share that intimacy for the first time. I think aside from anything superspiritual and the power of God to sustain us and keep us strong, we both just really want to enjoy the fullest expression of our love for the first time ever on our wedding night. I think that the anticipation of that keeps us from wanting to cheapen it. My fiancé and I do express our sexuality in different ways and are intimate in our times together. It's not a thing of seeing how close to the line we can go. It's loving each other and affirming that attraction and showing that. Holiness does not mean to ignore the attraction and desire for intimacy, but to express that in ways that honor one another and honor the Lord."
>
> Angie Yandell, twentysomething

Good sex is laying out in a hammock on a starry night. It's running to the Sonic Drive-In for their Butterfinger Blast. It's saying yes when you are tired on occasion because you know how much he truly needs that intimacy—with you and only you. It's setting aside one night a week for date night. It's appreciating your body and what it means to him, whether you are young and fit or if you've picked up a few pounds and stretch marks because you've carried his children. It's undressing in the light. Good sex for a lifetime with one man unfolds as you develop these traits together: *Relationship. Rapport.*

Bond. Understanding. Connection. Sensuality. These are words that bloom into reality when you nurture each other.

I'm not married yet

There is a reason that I didn't share the details of how to have great physical sex in the previous section. There are great faith-filled books devoted to that topic. But few speak of building a foundation of an awesome sex life or distinguishing between having sex and making love. You can build a foundation for great future sex now. It's choosing to have fun without adding the pressure of physical intimacy. If you are in a relationship, it's being kind to each other, building intimacy and attitudes toward each other that are deeper than physical. It's also genuine sensuality. What is that? It's a confident woman. It's appreciating how God made you, and understanding that one day your body will bring the right person pleasure, and you will find pleasure with him. It's working on who you are and what you love as you wait, whether you are in a relationship or not.

Waiting is difficult. The desire to be intimate is strong, not just because of the cultural standards, but because we are wired to be intimate. But while you wait, it's not a dormant period, but rather proactive. Jason Illian, in *Undressed: The Naked Truth About Love, Sex and Dating*, says,

> "Staying put" is about allowing our hearts to be still long enough for God to share his remarkable plan for our lives. It is about listening to the echo of emptiness within, learning the essence of true, sacrificial "'til death do us part" love, and applying it to our everyday relationships. God doesn't act like Santa Claus, gift-wrapping our spouses and leaving them in the living room for us to find after passionate prayer. He knows that for us to love completely, we must learn to love the Lord first and others second.[2]

It's no secret that "waiting" is considered out of date. The attitude toward virginity reminds me of the classic novel *The Scarlet Letter,* by Nathaniel Hawthorne. In a role reversal, if you are unmarried and a virgin, you might identify with these words: "Ah, but let her cover the mark as she will, the pang of it will be always in her heart."

Virginity isn't considered just old-school, but antiquated. But even if a man asks for less, you might consider asking for more. Camerin Courtney, in *The Unguide to Dating,* says, "It takes time, prayer, keen observation skills, and input from others you respect to figure out the true character of a potential date or mate."[3] You are waiting to make sure that the guy that you choose is the right man. You wait to get physically involved because sex should mean something. You wait so that your family tree does not have the jagged lines of estrangement or the pain of divorce. Maybe your extended family tree is already rife with these relationships, and they have affected you adversely, but how your family looks for you and your future children can be drastically altered as you wait for God's best.

I'm already in an unhealthy relationship, Suzie

Prayerfully take an unhealthy relationship to God. He's aware of your pain. He's aware of your love for another human being. And he's got the blueprints to your life; remember? He's also holding the blueprints to his life, and to the life of the man he intended to be with you. Get very real. If the relationship is physical only, are you willing to expect more? Paris Finner-Williams, in *Single Wisdom,* strongly advises women to stop doing permanent things with temporary partners. She writes, "To end or bring to a close unhealthy or unheavenly or just plain bad romantic relationship that you know is not from God, means to have a finished conclusion or reach an end."[4] In other words, close the door permanently.

Unhealthy relationships can take many forms. It can be the song and dance of a woman waiting patiently for years for a man to commit while putting her hopes of a family and a home on hold. It's sharing a man who refuses to be exclusive, though he gets all the benefits of exclusivity, because at least the woman has someone—or something—to hold on to. It's staying in verbally or physically abusive relationships when God intended a woman to be loved. It's becoming the "other woman"—settling for a half man because he promises he'll one day love only her instead of his wife and family. It's moving in together to try out a relationship because "most marriages fall apart anyway."

"Ninety percent of couples that live together say their relationship is 'on the rocks'—so most never even make it to the altar," says Pam Farrel. "Satan is such a deceiver. He wants us to give away freely without commitment that which is the most precious gift: our sexuality. The biggest lie today is, 'If you love someone, live together first to test-drive the relationship.' If there is one sure-fire way to wreck love, it is to live together. More and more people are doing it—and more and more we are seeing the pain."[5]

Vintage love

Perhaps you are one of the thousands who now say that they desire more traditional values in relationships. When I met my husband's granddad, he pulled me aside and whisked out a faded and cracked photo of his bride of 60 years. Grandmother Franklin no longer looked like that picture. She was bent over and aged. She was feisty and tart and loving. And he was still in love with her. He asked me to make a promise. "If you will love Richard just half as much as I love Hazel, you'll have a good life," he said.

Granddaddy Franklin passed away a few years ago. He died of a stroke after several years of illness. It was a slow and painful four years. Grandmother was his caretaker the entire time. It was

difficult to watch the strong man she fell in love with grow weak and unable to care for his smallest needs. Yet that love was strong until his death—and still burns in her heart today.

Do you long for this type of love? In *Notting Hill* with Julia Roberts and Hugh Grant, Julia delivers a line that strikes a chord: "I'm just a girl, standing in front of a boy, asking him to love her."

Waiting may be the difficult part in your quest for that love, but Romans 8 is encouraging:

> Waiting does not diminish us, any more than waiting diminishes a pregnant mother. We are enlarged in the waiting. We, of course, don't see what is enlarging us. But the longer we wait, the larger we become, and the more joyful our expectancy.

If you are in an unhealthy relationship, I pray that you will stop and reassess what you desire in love, and make the decisions that you must to bring you joy and security, for you are God's girl and he loves you deeply.

Is it even *possible* to have a good marriage?

What about healthy relationships? Where do you begin? With half of marriages dissolving, many wonder if a good marriage is possible. Scripture offers a picture of marriage in Ephesians 5:

> Out of respect for Christ, be courteously reverent to one another.
>
> Wives, understand and support your husbands in ways that show your support for Christ. The husband provides leadership to his wife the way Christ does to his church, not by domineering but by cherishing. So just as the church submits to Christ as he exercises such leadership, wives should likewise submit to their husbands.
>
> Husbands, go all out in your love for your wives, exactly as Christ did for the church—a love marked by giving, not

> getting. Christ's love makes the church whole. His words evoke her beauty. Everything he does and says is designed to bring the best out of her, dressing her in dazzling white silk, radiant with holiness. And that is how husbands ought to love their wives. They're really doing themselves a favor—since they're already "one" in marriage.
>
> No one abuses his own body, does he? No, he feeds and pampers it. That's how Christ treats us, the church, since we are part of his body. And this is why a man leaves father and mother and cherishes his wife. No longer two, they become "one flesh."

Unfortunately this scripture is often misunderstood or taken out of context. This chapter launched a flood of e-mails into my in-box: *What does it mean to submit? Is this something that makes sense in this century? How come so many people mess up the real meaning of this passage?*

Read these scriptures one more time—but first strip away cultural preconceptions. What you find is a picture of a man who loves his wife so much that he would give his life for her. He nurtures her above his own needs. He serves her. It's sacrificial love. His role is founded on his unselfish love toward his mate. It describes a woman who honors and respects her husband. She recognizes his wisdom, his leadership abilities, and his sacrificial love to her. She is at his side as his partner and they are one. This is not the type of relationship typically modeled in many marriages, but what would happen if it were?

Love and respect

A woman might think it weak—instead of strong—to submit. A man might see it as weak—instead of strong—to love sacrificially. But we all desire and need love and respect. In the book *For Young Women Only,* Shaunti Feldhahn and Lisa Rice surveyed several men, asking this question: Would you rather feel alone

and unwanted or inadequate and disrespected by everyone? Men replied that they would rather feel alone and unwanted than disrespected![6]

I struggled with that answer, so I asked my husband the same question. After all, he's a sensitive man. His answer surprised me. He said, "If I felt inadequate and disrespected, I'd feel alone and unwanted anyway."

> "I heard someone say once that in marriage God asked the man and woman to each do the one thing that was absolutely and totally foreign to them. For the man to love someone else as much as Christ loves his church (that is, to the point of death—not only physically but also figuratively); and for the woman to submit herself to another person and, essentially, trust another person with her life. I was either not yet married or fairly newly married when I heard that, and I remember thinking, *Gee, it really doesn't sound that hard.*"
>
> SARAH BALLARD, THIRTYSOMETHING

I'm one of the strongest, most independent women you'll ever meet, and that's not a bad trait. It is the way that God created me, and yet I fully embrace the true meaning of this passage. To submit means that I choose to honor the person that I married with sincere words that build him up. I will let him know that I love him. I will look for opportunities to speak highly of him in front of others. My words will not be used to demean or demoralize him. I also choose to believe that I am worthy of unselfish love. I will communicate my needs and show Richard what makes me feel safe and nurtured. I won't expect him to instinctively know what I desire, or need. I won't accept dominion or selfishness as love. This is a long-term commitment that we have made to each other. I can't manipulate him into doing his part, but I can do mine. The beauty is that he responds when I do, and with continual communication (not nagging, but sincere and open dialogue) I receive what I need from him. The longer we are married, the more this biblical foundation makes sense.

What about the bad times?

Richard worked in a factory for some years after we sold our farming business. The factory was hot and dirty and the work was demanding, and yet he remained there because it paid the bills. Because of my battle with cancer, we needed consistent income and insurance. Though he never complained, this job chipped away at Richard's spirit. In fact, at times I felt like I had lost the man I loved. He was present, but he fought mood swings so I felt alone as he sat quietly. I wanted to cry at our loss. He didn't smile or laugh like he once did, and when I asked him about his dreams, he shrugged his shoulders.

A marriage will ebb and flow, and that is when commitment matters. You work as a team to find solutions until the deep love you have for one another rises to the surface once again. You seek help, if you need help. I prayed for Richard. I prayed for myself, because I wasn't patient with this stranger. I wanted to shake him, make him move to another job...anything to find the joyful man I loved. I reminded myself that he was working so that my children and I could pursue our dreams. I rubbed his back while he slept at night, and prayed for him, choosing to be thankful for this precious man who didn't rage in spite of his feelings, but chose silence rather than hurt his loved ones with words. That period was the most difficult in our marriage, and things didn't change overnight. It was time for us to live our faith, rather than just profess to be moved by it. Richard needed me to believe for him even when he couldn't see his way past his feelings. I needed him to hear me, to listen to the heart of his wife and his lover. We needed to formulate a plan to move us beyond the stagnant place we were in. That season of our marriage seems very distant now, but how we chose to handle it was critical.

We took huge steps of faith together. Richard left his job five years later to pursue a counseling degree. It wasn't my timing. I was ready years before he was, but his wisdom and my ability to

dream meshed, and we made the decision together, and it became the right timing. The happy, lighthearted man I married returned to me, and I'm grateful.

When you marry, you will live in both the "for better or for worse" parts of marriage, but as you work together, respect each other, model love, patience, kindness to each other, and continue to love with God's help, your marriage can only grow stronger.

What do you bring to a relationship? List your strengths and your weaknesses.

____

____

What cultural messages have caused problems? What is one thing that you can do differently if you approach it spiritually?

____

____

When you read 1 Corinthians 13, are there areas where you need spiritual help? Write them down and then take a moment and ask God for direction and assistance.

____

____

If you redefine "waiting" to proactively building a foundation for future love, does it change the way you feel about waiting?

____

____

List one way that you wish to be nurtured. Have you communicated this (gently and with clear direction)?

If single, do you know what it means to be nurtured? Define it.

____

____

Heavenly Father, I thank you that you know how to love me perfectly. Help me to learn to love with excellence. Help me to share my needs, but also to be sensitive to the needs of the man in my life. I choose to pray for him daily and to be an encourager. I ask for your blessing over my relationship and my home.

For the single 20-something

God, let me love you while I wait for the right person. Help me to grow as your daughter, and to become an encourager to my friends and family—and to myself! Help me to recognize the man that will love me as you do, and to recognize those who will not. Thank you for your love and your direction in every area of my life, but especially in this area. I need you.

What happens when we live God's way?
He brings gifts into our lives, much the same way that fruit appears in an orchard—things like affection for others, exuberance about life, serenity. We develop a willingness to stick with things, a sense of compassion in the heart, and a conviction that a basic holiness permeates things and people. We find ourselves involved in loyal commitments.

FROM GALATIANS 5

Blog

Got a friendship manual?

Current mood: contemplative

Sometimes I wish there was a how-to manual for friendship, something tailor-made for me so I'd know exactly how to respond in each situation. I know that's impossible, but I feel like most people have this friendship thing down pat while I still struggle with some of its basic elements. I like connecting deeply with people, but I've recently realized I can be a friend in other ways without having to feel like it's second best. I can befriend others by just being someone to hang out with, bringing food, helping with a project, or praying for them. I've also learned to look for friendship in unexpected places.

After years of few friends and then finally coming to a church with many young women my age, I never dreamed that my closest friend there would be 20 years my senior. Though my friendships aren't perfect, I know I don't need a how-to book for them to be wonderful.

Katie Hart, twentysomething

FIVE

The friendship factor

ONE DAY I WAS PREPARING for a humanities test, driving young children to soccer practice, and teaching teens in a discipleship class. The next I was listening to the hum of the MRI machine while doctors looked for cancer in my body. I had just celebrated my thirty-second birthday. The news wasn't good, and friends and family had filled the room the next Monday after surgery.

My dad leaned over my hospital bed and whispered, "Just give me the word and I'll clear everybody out." He frowned at the crowd.

I listened to the beep of the monitor, watched the drip of the IV, and smiled at the knots of people standing in every available space. "I don't want them to leave, Dad," I whispered back. "I need them."

And I did.

My friends were more stunned than I by the diagnosis of cancer. They didn't know the right words to say, so they brought flowers and chocolate and cards. They brushed their hands across my hair. They cried. They told jokes that didn't make sense. They took my young children for lunch or to a movie and gave them all the love and assurance they knew to give. Friends mowed our lawn. They cleaned my house. They fixed food. They prayed. They hung posters in the hospital room with words of encouragement. They arrived for my chemo appointments when Richard was scheduled to work, and bravely sat with me while the nurse slipped the needle in my vein.

They also saved me from embarrassment. One day I walked out of the radiation dressing room and slipped past a dozen or so people in the small lobby. A friend ran after me, and I felt a hard tug as she jerked my skirt, which was tucked in my bikini underwear.

I needed them. Their love for me during that period showed me that they needed me too. They were willing to do what it took to keep me around. Nothing that my friends did can be found in a medical book, and yet every gesture and word brought healing. Before cancer, I could list the names of my friends, but during cancer I rediscovered the *meaning* of friendship.

A few years ago I realized that my friend time had dwindled to nothing. My friendships had changed. My theory was that my friendships would exist in a maintenance mode. Every 3000 miles or so, I injected a little oil—meeting by accident and catching up; meeting for a lunch or dinner date here or there. One weekend I prepared for a conference and started praying for the women who would be in attendance. As I prayed, faces of my closest friends came to mind, friends who were once a very intricate part of my life and now distant dots on the radar of my existence.

I replayed scenarios that kept us apart—children's activities, their jobs, my writing, attending different churches or living in different communities. But if I was honest, those things existed before and our friendships thrived. What had happened?

It was me. I was unavailable. *Maybe next month, would that be okay? It's crazy busy right now.* They called often. *Want to go to lunch? How about we get together Friday night and have a girls' night out?* In spite of their efforts, it appeared I had no room in my life for these relationships. There is a solitary streak in me that allows

me to be my own best friend. I love to cruise antique shops alone. I can snuggle with a great book and good music and be happy. I love spending time alone with my family.

But, I need friends. I need their encouragement. I need to be with women who challenge and motivate me, and who make me laugh. I need friends to talk with about things that only girlfriends love to talk about. I also need to be with people who are different from me. My lack of involvement with others created a personal bubble. Many friends and acquaintances were from my church, and our times together were in a faith-filled environment. I traveled to speak to people about faith, and these events were weekend conferences with large crowds and little personal interaction. The greater part of my day was spent working from a home office. I longed to have real conversations about faith and life with people who might not believe as I do. I wanted to hear their perspective, and perhaps share mine. It was time to re-evaluate the power of friendship—and to be a better friend.

Hey, girlfriend!

> *A good friend is not different than your child or a parent. You simply love them. But there are times when you can't talk to a parent or child because they are too close to the situation, but you can talk to a friend and they see the situation from the outside looking in. That's the difference.*
>
> TAMMI STEELE, SUZIE'S FORTYSOMETHING FRIEND

Women are created for intimacy. By nature we are nurturers and comforters. We love to love one another. We love to communicate. You will rarely see women talk like men. We don't invite each other to check out our cars' engines. We don't feel weird if we hug or touch. We don't touch, scratch, or adjust our private areas at any time during our conversation! Instinctively we want to go deep. We want details. We want to get real and talk about things that matter, and we want to be a part of each other's lives. What is a friend? She is someone you feel close to, see often, and can count on, and it's so much greater than surrounding yourself with acquaintances. Because women are built for intimacy, you and I can run empty when we surround ourselves only with co-workers, or online friendships, or perhaps just our own company.

> "I never thought my definition of friendship would change so much. I'm figuring out that my old childhood definition of friendship is no longer applicable today. When I was younger, I thought I would have the same friends always. The friends that I thought I could count on through everything are no longer there. I used to think a friend was someone to see and hang out with, but I've learned that my friends are people that guide me spiritually, let me lean on them in times of trouble, rejoice with me when I have victories. I believe that God brings people in and out of your life for certain reasons, but I believe that God brings true friends in your life to help guide you along."
>
> Michelle Plunkett, twentysomething

Friendship allows you to communicate, and it brings companions into your life. But there is a surprising third "C" in the mix of friendship. In John 15, Jesus said to his disciples, "This is my *command:* Love one another the way I loved you." Jesus had every heavenly resource available to him, yet he chose a few close friends to be his confidants. He drew strength from them. He gave and received encouragement and fellowship with those in his inner circle. In his darkest hours, right before he would be betrayed and led to death upon a cross, he took three of his best friends with him to pray. These men didn't know that Jesus would soon suffer, but they willingly went along with him, though they were tired.[1]

By example, Jesus shows the power of intimate friendship.

Friendships change in your 20s

As you hit your 20s and 30s the nature of friendships change. The circle of acquaintances (co-workers, neighbors, and so on) grows while the community of deep relationships narrows to include close friends. In high school you perused the joys of relationships in classes, hallways, and school events. College is also an incubator for close relationships, but it gets tougher to hold on to close relationships with friends when you add ingredients to your life such as responsibility, work, distance, or family.

Priorities also change and you realize, that just like any other relationship, deep friendships take effort. As those relationships change, these three keys may be helpful to maintain close relationships:

1. Friendship is sacrificial.
2. Friendship is a gift.
3. Friendship requires commitment.

> "My freshman year of college was a difficult one for me. In many ways I was ready to conquer the world, but deep in my heart I felt fear and inadequacy. There were so many people who knew exactly what they wanted in life and made it a point to conquer their goals every day. Those people made me nervous and out of place. My biggest concern was, 'How am I going to pay my school bill?' Yes, I had big dreams, but they seemed to fade in the sight of reality.
>
> "During this time of emotional concern and worry, I found myself sitting in my room alone and having no desire to make new friends. I didn't like the feeling of newness. I just wanted to go home, back to my life of comfort. One day I was crying about making friends and the Lord gently spoke to me, 'Crystal, you can stay in your room crying, or you can make a choice and go out there and meet people.' It was so simple and so true."
>
> CRYSTAL HAHN, TWENTYSOMETHING

Friendship takes work

John Leonard, an Australian poet, once said, "It takes a long time to grow an old friend."

A few years back, one of my friends was struggling. Until that time our friendship was easy. We made time for each other. Being with her was always fun. But then things started going wrong with an important relationship. I wanted to "fix" her situation.

More than that, I wanted to fix *us*. I finally realized that she wasn't asking me to fix anything. She wanted someone to love her and to talk with when the timing was right. She wasn't looking for me to act as Superwoman and fly in with all the answers. I dropped a card and small gift by her job. I prayed for her. Soon, she realized that I had retired my cape and that I was prepared to be a friend instead of trying to manage her difficulties. It allowed her the freedom to be open about her feelings.

She knew that I would take them into a private place of prayer and give them to someone much bigger than I, and leave them there. My good friend Tammi Steele defines friendship this way: "A good friendship is knowing each other's heart and being there for each other—especially in the difficult times."

Maintaining close relationships take a little more work than it did before adulthood. It's not only being sensitive to each other, but it's making time, which is especially difficult if you're juggling a thousand different things. It might be sending a card, or text messaging just to let her know she's on your mind. Another close friend, RaNaile Clymer, and I have been good friends for several years. We have celebrated with each other, cried with one another, and yet keeping that relationship close continues to take work due to distance and to our different schedules. As I wrote this book I asked her what she needed from me as a friend. She said, "To me, a true friend is someone who you know will always be there no matter how much distance is between you—or someone you know will forgive you when you don't take the time to make that call, and when you do make that call, you just pick up the conversation as if it had been yesterday. And I have that with you."

I will work on my relationships with my best friends because

they matter. They will change, and there may be times that I make sacrificial effort to grow an "old friend."

A recent study says that friendship is worth the effort, stating that friends increase your enjoyment of life! According to this study, good friendships relieve moments of loneliness and reduce stress. When you are socially isolated, it takes a toll on your physical and mental heath. The study stated that friendship serves as a buffer, protecting against various ills, including depression, high blood pressure, clogged arteries, infections, and even death.[2]

Quick! Grab a friend!

Online vs. face-to-face interaction

This morning I checked my blogs, MySpace, and my e-mail. I list these contacts in the back because it's a great way to connect with new friends, and sometimes online friendships—a sassier version of your grandparents' front porch—are the most convenient relationships. But you and I need face-to-face interaction. Online relationships allow you to drop in, leave a comment, or meet new people and then resume life as normal. It's difficult to know someone from text alone. A mental image is developed, and meeting in person can be surprising. Or those who you know face-to-face can become online-only buddies.

Face-to-face conversation distinguishes the difference between acquaintances and true friends. If you unplugged for a month, it's likely that your circle of friends would diminish quickly. Communication would continue with genuine friends, even if it isn't convenient. Face-to-face relationships allows you a healthy outlet to discuss things that matter to you. When surveyed, most Americans said that they could only name two people with whom they could discuss matters of personal importance, according to a survey of nearly 1500 adults published in June in the journal, *American Sociological Review.* Less than one of these is a friend outside the family. One in four people surveyed said they had no confidant at all.[3]

The gift of friendship

I love hanging out with Richard. And yet I need friends as well. Friendship doesn't replace the other parts of your life, or the other people in your life, but it does enrich them. A great friendship allows you to nurture that part of you that is not student, daughter, ministry leader, employee, mommy, or wife. These are all serious aspects of friendship, but a good friend can be enriching or just be plain fun. Just for fun, let's see what a great friendship looks like:

1. You don't need a special occasion to get together.
2. You can pig out together—and then go swimsuit shopping.
3. She sees more in you then what you see in the mirror.
4. She brings a casserole and scrubs your bathroom when you are sick.
5. You can eat off each other's plate.[4]
6. She is there when you are in the "bad things happen to good people" part of your life.
7. She alerts you when you're heading for the guy who looks great but is a loser.
8. She accepts you for who you are but isn't afraid to appreciate your abilities and challenge you to soar beyond your limitations.
9. She tells you the truth when you need to hear it—and offers you chocolate afterward.
10. She tells you when you have spinach in your teeth.[5]

If you have a friend like this, then she is a gift. If you are a friend like this, then you are a friend worth keeping. When we realize that friendship is a gift, we embrace it, cherish it, and take good care of the relationship.

The big reveal

There are three reasons you might not want to commit to friendship: 1) You are intimidated. 2) You've been hurt. 3) You want to avoid the big "reveal."

She doesn't look like me. She doesn't have the same interests. She's more talented, successful, spiritual. She's an artist. She's a mom and wife, and I'm not married yet. Just like the woman who creates a stringent list for her future mate, many women create a set of standards for their friends. That's great, as long as you don't use them to avoid meeting someone different than you. My best friend, Vera Epperson, shared this with me, "I can honestly count the friendships that I have had. I'm not sure if that is good or bad, but I will say that I don't think you can call any of them a chance meeting. I have learned something from them all. I have grown, and even climbed out of my comfort zone a few times. True friends laugh with you, cry with you, and always look past who you are to what you can become. Maintaining friendships? This is where I need to pick up the pace. I believe it starts with commitment, just like spending time with God and keeping that relationship strong. It is very important to always make time for your friends."

Take a moment and think about your friends. What new qualities do they add to your life, or are they all reproductions of you? Sometimes God draws you to people who are different for a reason. They have the same passion or a quality that you wish you had. A friend may be in a different place in life than you—more advanced in her career, more mature spiritually, or happily pregnant. She may come from a different place and have unique customs or approach life from a different angle. Those differences can be a catalyst in your life and help you reach beyond what you've called "normal" before.

A few months ago I started serving with other women in my community in a program called the 20-10 Challenge. I meet with

25 to 30 fascinating women three to four times a month as we mentor freshmen girls in high school. Not only did it reward my love for teens and my desire to see girls grow as women, but it introduced me to a diverse group of women, who were leaders in many different ways—whether business or politics or visionaries in other areas. It also launched me out of my comfort zone! Though we are diverse in our belief systems, faith comes up naturally in conversations that involve real-life matters. My new friends know my heart. They know that my faith is genuine and trust that what I am saying is truth—at least to me—and will listen because they understand that I have no hidden agendas.

Think about the possibilities! Is there a woman that you've excluded because you are intimidated? Perhaps you might consider broadening your friendship list to include her, or expanding your friendship base to include people with different interests and backgrounds.

My last friend hurt me

Dee Brestin, in her book *Friendships of Women,* describes women as roses. They are beautiful, but they have thorns. Gardeners love roses because they bring beauty in their gardens, but they realize when they are jabbed by a thorn that the rose had no personal animosity toward them; they were simply born with thorns. The master gardeners learn how to handle the roses so they won't get jabbed! Years ago I had a friend who had thorns. She was younger by a few years, and her thorn was jealousy. This pervaded many areas of her life. She was mistrustful of other women around her husband, as friends, and even as co-workers. I was unsure of how to handle this jealousy. Other than this thorn she was intelligent, fun, and a great person. One day she called me and was expressing her anger at a woman who had looked at her husband the wrong way. I was as gentle as I knew to be,

but I was honest. Her jealousy was not only misdirected, it was destructive. Her response surprised me:

"I hate being jealous and I want to change. Why didn't you tell me this before? How can I learn from you as a friend if you aren't honest with me?"

Good question. Friends are truthful with each other. But before you approach them, perform a heart check—both for your friend and yourself. What is her motivation? What drives that behavior or flaw in your friend? Be open about the problems in your friendship and promise to work together to resolve them. My friend was raised in a home where she strived hard to gain attention. That produced insecurity that ran deep. On the outside everything looked whole, but on the inside she was still looking for security and was jealous of anyone who threatened what she had worked so hard to achieve, so she built a protective wall of jealousy.

I wasn't my friend's counselor, and it wasn't my place to diagnose or demand change. But recognizing those walls allowed me to be first compassionate and then honest with her. In my book *The Mom I Want to Be,* I described the walls that women build:

> The funny thing about walls is, they often look nice on the outside. We dress them up, masking them with a smile, with politeness, or a polished exterior. We might even win awards for our walls, but underneath the facade, a cracked fortress resides around our heart and soul. As women, we are perhaps the finest craftsmen of walls. They serve as a shelter; as long as we remain inside we avoid further hurt or exposure. They mask vulnerability. The armed guard at the wall is you because that is the only person you trust.[6]

Perhaps you've been hurt by a friendship and have built your own protective barriers to keep intruders safely on the outside.

There are no risk-free ventures in friendship, but there are possibilities. Are you willing to chip away at that wall today?

There *are* instances where a person's motivation is intentional and hurtful. If a friend's presence in your life is destructive to your purpose, your relationship with God, or with family members, then it's time to flee. These are women who want to tear down your relationships with other friends, family, or God. That's a danger zone that says, "I'm not willing to respect or honor what is valuable to you," and that's not a true friend.

> "I think we were created for community and Satan does everything he can to put us in a place of isolation. Even in the very beginning he came to Eve to challenge her in her independence. He didn't tempt Adam and Eve together, but waited until she was most vulnerable. He hasn't changed his game plan in all these years. He loves to isolate us. He loves the fact that if we're not around others who speak life into us, we can easily embrace his lies about our future, our appearance, and our character. He gets joy out of making us feel completely alone. The way to jack Satan and his plan is to be around others, it challenges your way of thinking, grows your character and ultimately the more you relate to people the more you learn about the vastness of God. So to me friends are a vital part of my life."
>
> CRYSTAL HAHN, TWENTYSOMETHING

No pretending with good friends

Perhaps the biggest fear of letting down our walls is the "Big Reveal." Suddenly people will see you for who you are. There's no pretending with good friends. To avoid that moment when people will see past the façade, many women busy themselves with other things, and are immersed in activities but isolated from deep relationships.

Friendship requires vulnerability. You take off the mask to be real with another human being. Some dictionaries define *vulnerable* as "weak" or "helpless." That's a definition that many use to avoid friendships with other women. But I love this definition: "open" or "open to." Friendships allow you to open your heart

to another person. *But what if they don't accept me?* If someone doesn't accept you for who you are, then right around the corner will be someone who will.

Your 20s is a time of transition. Perhaps this is an area where you desire to strengthen old relationships, or forge new ones. Take a moment and share your thoughts.

Are you open to friendship? Why or why not?

____

____

Are you willing to be vulnerable and strip away the pretenses?

____

____

Are you a good friend? Why or why not? What is one thing you would like to change?

____

____

How important is friendship? List the things that get in the way of having a close friend.

____

____

Name your top three friends. Make a date to spend time with them. Send a friend a note. Do something that will show your friends that they are on your mind. (List these beside your friends' names.)

____

____

Jesus, you needed friends. In your darkest hours you shared your heart with those closest to you. You loved fully. You laughed. I want to be a good friend to others, but also need diverse friends in my life. Lead me to a good friend. If I have walls built around my heart, climb inside those walls with me and help me to break them down.

Friends come and friends go,
but a true friend sticks by you like family.
FROM PROVERBS 18

Blog

Far from home

Current mood: hopeful

I'm seven months into this journey and most of the time I feel like I have no more direction than I did a year ago. Sometimes even to the point of questioning, "Did I hear you correctly, Jesus? Am I truly where I'm supposed to be?" In my heart I really do know that I am supposed to be here. Why exactly? I have no idea. Maybe that comes in the waiting. I was told before I even moved, from someone I respected and loved, that I would pretty much fail. That this would be a mistake. Those words haunt me sometimes. But then I look at what God has created, and the things I've been able to be involved in, but most of all the people I have met along the way.

I think about the people who have become my family. Truly remarkable people who I am honored to call my friends. People who teach me all the time how to be more like Christ. The more I reflect, the more I am reminded that even though I can't even see my hand in front of my face at times, God has shown me time and time again that I have to trust Him. I don't know how I'm going to get to where I want to go from here. I really don't, but I've learned the hard way that I will fail, if I try to do it on my own. I think I'm independent. I know I can make it. I'm a grown woman with a BA degree and mind of my own. I can handle it.

But through circumstances, I have discovered that I am afraid to depend on other people. I'm afraid to tell people that love and care about me that I'm struggling. Or that I'm doubting. I'm human. Not superhuman. And no one expects me to be superhuman. No one asks that of me, especially God. So, I find myself in a strange place. But I'm able to celebrate friends. I realize how awesome it is to be part of a family of faith. Who knows where we'll all go? Life will take us here and there. Some of us far away, but we can be linked in heart and spirit as we work towards a common goal.

Jess Saunders, twentysomething

SIX

Who is my community?

I KEPT MY HEAD DOWN, hoping the girls that walked on the backs of my flip-flops would go away. I was in Houston, visiting my biological father. I had met him only twice in my life. I was there to try to connect with him, but only because I felt I had no other place to go.

I slipped out of the house that day to walk to the local convenience store. I bought a frozen drink, and as I exited I saw a group of girls walk around the corner toward me. They looked tough, their shoulders high, swaggering down the street. I looked like myself—skinny and vulnerable. They marched behind me, approaching closer until they were tripping me from behind. I couldn't ignore the intimidation, so I turned.

"What do you want?" I pulled my purse tight.

"Give me a drink," one said. She smirked. Her friends laughed.

I was 17. I didn't know what to do. I looked around. I saw a woman peeking out her front door. She shut it quickly.

"I'm not hurting you," I said. "I don't even know who you are."

The larger girl grabbed at me. "Give me your drink." Another reached for my purse. I panicked and tossed my strawberry-peach frozen drink in the first girl's face.

Bad move. Bad, bad move.

A few minutes later I searched the sky as I lay on my back on the concrete. My purse was gone. My money was gone. A ring that I wore on my finger—a treasured gift from a friend—was stripped off my hand. I scraped myself off of the sidewalk and checked for injuries. I found only a few scuffs and bruises. I ran to a nearby house. The woman who had peeked out the front door moments earlier ignored my shouts for help as I banged on the door.

I felt so far from home—in more ways than one.

I was independent long before I was ready. I didn't know where to go, or who to trust. I was in Houston for a month to meet my biological father. The day that I was mugged I felt as abandoned as I ever had in my life. I had my faith and knew that I could turn to God, but I wanted someone with "skin on."

I didn't really know my father. Even as I stayed at his home, I felt like a visitor at a stranger's house. Not because he and his family weren't gracious, because they were, but there was no history, no connection. It was awkward, me showing up on their doorstep after all of these years. At that time, my family—the one I grew up in—was fractured. Another reason I was in Houston at 17 years of age.

Today I have a strong community. I know where to turn in case of emergency. I have found my "skin-on" family, and it is broader and more diverse than I ever realized. You see, family has taken on several shades of meaning. It is my husband's family. It is the family I grew up in. It is Richard, Ryan, Leslie, Melissa, Josh, and Stephen. It is my church. It is people in my city and people with whom I share similar passions. It is a group of women across the nation who write books and speak. My personal community is built on kinship with many different people and in many different ways.

Who is your community?

> *What makes a difference for twentysomethings who grow in their faith and one who grows stagnant or falls away? Without fail, relationships and community are most often cited as the determining factors for growth.*[1]
>
> MARGARET FEINBERG, AUTHOR OF *TWENTYSOMETHING*

As twentysomethings, you have left (or are leaving) the familiar world of family. You are creating new communities and the word *family* takes on a different meaning. I am the mother of three beautiful twentysomethings. Family is just as important to them as it always was, but as they crossed the threshold to adulthood they found new sources of strength and encouragement. My daughter Melissa and her husband, Josh, married two years ago. In the beginning, Melissa called me when she was sick or if she needed advice. She and Josh consulted us as they made big decisions. But within a short time, they put their trust in each other first. I'm grateful, for that is the way it should be. As my older daughter, Leslie, began her marriage journey with my brand-new son-in-law, Stephen, they did the same, turning toward each other to create their own family.

My son, Ryan, is connected to his Lambda Chi fraternity brothers. They bonded as men and not only wear the letters of brotherhood, but have proved to be a powerful source of community for Ryan. Today, as he nears completion of his master's program, these men remain friends, and continue to play a large role in his life. In the past, when a significant relationship didn't work out as he had hoped, these men wrapped around him with strength. The reality is that we all need people with skin on. I'm not offended by the fact that my grown children have established personal communities. It's a vital step toward independence.

Community is different from friendship. It's becoming a part of something larger. You contribute. You take. You work together. These people matter to you. You're diverse, but you also share common interests and passions. Together, you have the opportunity to make a difference. Building community is vital because your twenties can be a lonely time. You live independently, and sometimes it's rough out there. Loneliness is one thing that "they" failed to mention when talking about how wonderful it is to be on your own. Colin Creel, in *Perspectives: A Spiritual Life Guide for Twentysomethings* says, "Many decisions you make in your twenties affect the rest of your life for better or worse. Ironically, none of us are truly prepared or equipped to make those decisions."[2] This is where community can assist you, but finding it can prove complicated.

> "I think family is more complicated in your twenties. I have always been close to my family, but I have a hard time finding the time I need to spend with them. I'm trying to go to school and work, and balance all the things in my life. I'm still working on this."
>
> Tiffany Hammonds, twentysomething

The challenges of building community

Many of you left home a few years ago and you pay the bills and are self-sufficient. Others are on the fast track in your career, or you're establishing your dreams. Some of you are parents or are married and you own a house. You juggle motherhood and work or stay at home as a full-time mom. Some of you are students and you live in a dorm or share an apartment. You wash laundry on weekends at your parents' home. You scrape by as you juggle a part-time job, study, and social life.

Challenge #1: family ties

Each of you is in various phases of independence, and yet the ability to stand on your own as a twentysomething is a powerful pull. Even as the world recognizes your independence, your parent(s) might struggle. In some ways, this doesn't change. Though I've raised three children, have been married for over a quarter of a century, and travel around the world alone, my mother will scold me if I visit her and don't wear a thick enough coat. It used to bother me, but now I see that this is the way that she cares for me. It's hard for a parent to switch gears, and sometimes they don't see you the way that others do, for when you visit them it is in the familiar world in which they parented you.

They don't see you in your job. They don't hear or perceive how others view you. Their perspective hasn't expanded yet to include the adult you. They might remain in a rescue mode, inherently ingrained in them when you were five years old and ignored the childproof cap on the grape-flavored cold medicine.

> "Sometimes I genuinely wish that someone would hold my hand and tell me which way to go. But other times I realize that the latter isn't what I want so much at all. Maybe I do fall flat on my back sometimes, but I get back up again and I'm learning."
>
> Annie Zlomke, twentysomething

This can cause problems in the relationship, and you might find yourself pulling back just when you need family the most. Embracing adulthood doesn't mean that family ties are severed; they simply change. It may be that change takes place on your side of the relationship first. Don't hesitate to ask for advice when you need it, but be willing to listen if you ask. You can take the nuggets that apply to you or your situation and learn from their experience. You can thank them for their help, but show them that you are able to take care of things on your own. It may take time for the adult–adult relationship to emerge. This is an age-old waltz that most people must dance.

When you lived at home, your biological family might have been your major source of community. But things change. When you go home, you find yourself playing the familiar role of little sister, or labeled as "the messy one" long after it's true. You may be married or a parent or making six figures (or four), but no matter how much you've accomplished, there's still that parent/child dynamic lurking in conversations and interactions. Perhaps you receive advice for questions you have not asked, or suggestions that don't fit in the world in which you live. And yet you *need* family. Christine Hassler writes in *20-Something, 20-Everything,* "On one hand it is liberating not to have anyone tell us what to do. On the other, we yearn for someone to give us answers and guidance."[3]

> "I've learned that my parents want to know generally what is happening in my life because they care. Granted, there are still times—though I'm married, have two children, and am totally independent of my parents—that I have to remind my dad that he no longer needs to worry about me. But I also know, especially that I am now a parent, that he will always be my dad and will always react to me like my dad. Worrying about me and wanting to help me 'fix' my problems is a part of who he is. There is a part of me that finds this very special."
>
> Sarah Ballard, thirtysomething

This is when many twentysomethings decide that their extended family is not their first choice of community for a number of reasons. It's not that you don't love them; you do. Every person desires a pat on the back, or to know that someone is praying. There are times when we all want to let our guard down and share that we're lonely or unsure.

If your parents still see you as a child, invite them into your adult world. When I am requested to join my twentysomething children in their environment, I get to see different aspects of their personality as I see them through others' eyes. My perception of them grows beyond mother/child.

Challenge #2: embracing the title "adult"

Consider carefully whether your parents are the only ones who are keeping the ties to childhood firmly intact. Recently my pastor shared the news of an upcoming mission trip. "If you are an adult and have been on a mission trip with this church, will you stand up?" he asked.

I stood. Alone. I was surrounded by people in their 20s, and at least half had traveled overseas multiple times, building houses or serving on medical mission teams. One guy rose to his feet, but sat back down with uncertainty when no one else joined him.

"Why didn't you stand?" I whispered to a couple of friends next to me after I sat down.

"He said, 'If you are an *adult,*'" the 24-year-old woman whispered back.

In the way she whispered it, it sounded lethal, menacing with negative overtones. *Decrepit. Ancient.* Adult wasn't necessarily a certain age, but definitely not her. It had to be describing the older people in the building. My friend's point of view is that the word *adult* is maligned. Word associations are powerful, imprinting ways of thinking upon our consciousness. When my friend uttered the word *adult,* I heard the word association of "boring" and "old," and yet some of the most beautiful, purpose-filled women I know left the zip code of their 20s a long time ago, for being old truly is a state of mind. They are 40, and 50, and 60 and beyond, pursuing their dreams and touching the lives of others in a multitude of ways.

Have you embraced the definition of adulthood? Is it something that you've shared and/or demonstrated with your parents, cutting the ties of childhood, while establishing the new relationships that are adult-to-adult?

Challenge #3: when there aren't parents

Depending upon your family situation, you may not have the

luxury of turning to a parent, but are there surrogate parents that you trust and respect to advise you or pray for you? Including them on your adult journey can provide community right when you need it most. Richard and I are honored to be a part of community to a number of twentysomethings. We receive messages: *Pray for me. I'm not sure what I'm supposed to do; can you listen? I'm not sure what step to take next, any advice?*

We don't have all the answers, but most of the time they are just looking for someone to listen. As they unload the burden, most of the time they already have the solution, and just need to clarify it for themselves.

Challenge #4: I can't find a church

What about a church? New challenges! The church family in which you grew up—the one that you attended since you were in diapers—is two states away. It doesn't make sense to keep calling it your home church when you've lived elsewhere for five or ten years. But it's familiar. It's where you cut your spiritual teeth. But when you do go home, things have changed. The teens look like little kids, because they are. The service is geared toward families. The singles group is filled with 40-something guys looking for a date. So you return home, determined to find a vibrant, committed group of believers who aren't afraid of talking about living a life of faith in your world. This takes commitment, and it takes courage to walk into a new church to try to figure out where you fit, or if you fit. Once you do find a church community, it takes guts to get involved, especially if you are doing it on your own, for you are the visitor now.

None of these are excuses for not finding a church community, but rather realities for many twentysomethings. There are hundreds of great churches and it is vital that you have some type of spiritual community. You need others to walk with you as you make critical life decisions.

What about God, Suzie? Isn't he supposed to be my community?

He is, but thankfully he also draws you to those with skin on. Community is...

1. positive interaction within a group of people
2. voluntary
3. sharing your passion with others

Thriving community

If you were to peek at the past and view the disciples in action, you would discover a thriving community. They were a diverse crowd of men and women. Some people think that the 12 men Jesus selected to work closely with him were the only disciples, but a disciple was anyone who was a student of Jesus. These men and women were bound by a passion to share the message that the risen Christ was the Messiah, and to discover what part they played in that endeavor. Kelly Monroe Kullberg, in her book *Finding God Beyond Harvard,* writes,

> I was in awe that so few could do so much with so little when inspired by the love of the Holy Spirit. They reminded me of a group of once-cowardly and barely functional friends—some fishermen, a doctor, some hospitable women, a tax collector, a tentmaker—who later shaped the course of human history after encountering the resurrected Jesus.[4]

This community was much like one match lighting another, and flames of faith were the result. This resulted in extraordinary feats. The sick were healed. The eyes of the blind were opened. They endured persecution and misunderstanding by their neighbors, their church, and their government, but they also drew strength from one another. This happened in the ordinary. They opened their homes; they prayed; they hung out and ate fish and barley bread. In the book of Acts, Judas, Silas, Paul, and

Barnabus are on a road trip to Antioch. They've braced themselves for the reception. They expect to be judged and perhaps even falsely imprisoned or tortured. In Acts 15, it reports,

> On arrival, they gathered the church and read the letter. The people were greatly relieved and pleased. Judas and Silas, good preachers both of them, strengthened their new friends with many words of courage and hope. Then it was time to go home. They were sent off by their new friends with laughter and embraces all around to report back to those who had sent them...Paul and Barnabas stayed on in Antioch, teaching and preaching the Word of God. But they weren't alone.

They found strength from each other. Just a short time later, Paul and Barnabas were hauled into prison. When they were released, where did they go? Right back to their source of strength—their community. They encouraged each other and found what they needed to continue their ministry. Like cool water, community refreshed them, and they refreshed others.

Community is voluntary

In your 20s, community becomes what you create. For some, the biological family remains a primary community. Others honor family ties, but their community becomes four or five couples, or several friends, or a group of like-minded people with whom they remain connected and close. The secret is that one community does not take away from the other. When I am home I find rejuvenation as I walk down the halls of my home church. In ministry, I teach. I listen. I counsel and pray with others all weekend. When I fly home I may be tired emotionally, and yet something happens when my church community wraps their arms around me, glad to see me. I sit and bask in the service and I get filled back up. I'm among friends. I am there by choice.

You are free to decide who you want to grow with. How exciting is that? But that puts responsibility right back in your control. Are you unhappy because your familiar support system is no longer working, or you don't know where to begin, and yet the real question is, what are you doing to find new connections right where you are right now? As you build and redefine your community, here are two options to consider as you begin that process:

> "I feel that a reason that a lot of twentysomethings feel lack in their spiritual life, friendships, and fulfillment of their purpose is because they neglect to build community. It's not a choice, but a priority of a person following the way of Jesus. We must be willing to walk in community—even when it is hard; even when we've been hurt by someone; even when we feel the church is going in a different direction than we are. When you do that, than there is a deep sense of fulfillment and adventure and love. And love is really what we are all looking for."
>
> JAMIE SCHNEIDER, TWENTYSOMETHING

1. Search for community.
2. Serve in a community.

Search until you find it

A recent report from the Barna groups stated that many twentysomethings leave their faith for a season, only to come back when they are more "established." There are lots of reasons that have been suggested for this phenomenon, but perhaps one reason is the difficulty of finding a church community. I've grieved over twentysomething friends who desire a faith-based community and who need community as they make important life decisions, but who fade out of sight because they don't know where they fit anymore.

There can be a wasteland between the involvement you once had, and walking through the doors of a new church, knowing no one. Life gets complicated and plugging into a church community seems difficult. But it's no less vital. Let's just acknowledge that it's harder in your 20s. You are busier, you might be working weekends or long hours, taking finals, or in transition. Let's also be clear that there are churches that fail to realize how great the need is during this time of your life, that their programs are aimed at teens or families, and they might have a college and career Sunday school class, but nothing else.

But let's also acknowledge that God has a place for you in a faith-based community. Keep searching; keep asking God for direction until you find it. Perhaps you are one of the lucky ones and there are churches in your city that have created a worship experience suited just for you, but if not, keep looking until you find a church where you can become involved. Ask God to help you discover where you can get involved, and what you can bring to a faith-based community.

It's okay if it doesn't look like a traditional church. It may be a home-based cell group, or a thriving college ministry, or a twentysomething church that meets on Saturday night. It might be a group of friends meeting to discuss Scripture once a week. Or perhaps it *is* a traditional church and you connect with older and younger people who love God. None of the New Testament churches had a sign over the door or mailed out a bulletin. The church was people! Hebrews 10 urges us, "Let's see how inventive we can be in encouraging love and helping out." The Christian faith began with Jesus and a small group of students of his teaching. From those few, the church grew from house to house and town to town. In those gatherings people helped one another understand and live the Christian life. Jesus made the statement, "When two or three of you are together because of me, you can be sure that I'll be there."[5] He was reinforcing the truth that to be his follower and to grow in faith, involvement with others is necessary.

The church was interdependent. They contributed their gifts and resources. They built one another up. They worshiped together. That still defines a faith-based community. It's more

than sitting alone on a pew. It's more than having your name on a mailing list. It's bonding with others who believe. It's digging together in the Word to build your faith. It's praying for each other. As one of the proverbs says, "You use steel to sharpen steel, and one friend sharpens another."[6] You may have to redefine your definition of "church." You may have to take a bigger look at what you can offer to a community. You take risks in relationships. You take risks as you choose your career. Are you willing to take risks to build your personal faith community?

You find community when you serve

My friend Jill Rigby is a fiftysomething Southern girl. She's had to establish new communities several times in her life. When she was in her mid-20s she moved from Mississippi to Manhattan. She says, "I haven't lived near family since I graduated from high school and yet, I've never felt alone." When she moved from the South to the East, she encountered culture shock. But as soon as she arrived she began to search for community. "Within three weeks of putting my feet on the concrete," she says, "I volunteered at the Museum of American Folk Art. Because of my longstanding passion, I didn't want to miss an opportunity to be in the midst of my favorite genre of art." Jill loves to serve, and this became a source of community to her. There were additional benefits. She couldn't afford the price of tickets for the functions that the museum sponsored, but as a volunteer she participated in most of them, and she met more interesting people.

Jill advises, "Volunteer wherever you find yourself. You not only render a valuable service, but you meet folks you wouldn't otherwise." This is more than words. Jill lived in one small town for only three months and taught Vacation Bible School. She was in North Carolina for an extended stay and painted clay pots with a charming older woman she met. Even if she is in a city for one week, Jill will find someone that she can serve. "Service to others is the antidote to being alone. Isn't that what Christ was trying to help us understand when He told us we must lay down our lives to find our lives?"

Today Jill lives in Louisiana. She works with children in schools through a program she developed, called "Manners of the Heart." When Hurricane Katrina devastated neighboring cities, she was pivotal in reaching out to children. She continues in her 50s to live out the biblical example of building community through serving.

Intertwine your passion with others

By nature I'm an introvert, but as opportunities to speak unfolded, I prepared by reading books, studying the Bible, seeking biblical answers so that I could share messages in a relevant manner. I pray over each event, and continue to sharpen my craft. I am supported and encouraged by many, especially Richard and my adult children. People at my church are excited that I travel, and often commit to pray for me. But my role as a speaker is often a lonely one. At my house, I am Richard's wife and I love that role. I am mom, another beautiful part of my life. My family is one of my strongest communities. My church is as well, but at church I am a discipleship teacher, a friend.

Inside these communities, there are few that I know of who are passionate about speaking, so when I talk about it, which is rare, it seems exciting—traveling, meeting new people, getting paid for speaking. So I don't express the challenges, such as being away from family, spending time in airports or nights in a hotel alone. I don't talk about the criticism received because I'm paid for a "one-hour talk," though that one hour is actually two full days of travel, several hours spent preparing a message, handouts, and material, and lots of prayer and preparation. I don't share that many times my family takes a financial hit because I know I'm supposed to speak somewhere and the costs are greater than the compensation. I don't say that there are times I struggle when I receive feedback

with 100 glowing comments, but that one that says, "Not worth the cost of registration, don't know why I came."

Speaking *is* a privilege, and I will do it with joy as long as I am allowed, but as in any ministry or career or endeavor, there are positive and negative facets. Five years ago I discovered the Advanced Writers and Speakers Association (AWSA). It is a group of over 200 faith-filled women from all over the nation who travel, speak, and write. When I attended the first conference, I sat quietly as I drank in every word. These women *understood.* I stay in touch through an online group, and we meet once a year for a professional conference. Many are close friends. AWSA is not my primary community, but it is an important group of people to me. It allowed me to bond with women who not only "get it," but who know how to stir the flames of a united passion.

Are you part of a community who will be your fire-starter? Have you looked for those who love music, cooking, youth ministry, foreign languages, or wherever your enthusiasm lies? If not, where can you begin today?

You will gain confidence as you take risks to build community. Life becomes a series of possibilities as you choose new friends and build future relationships. Are you ready to take a deeper look at perhaps the weaknesses and strengths of your personal community?

Who is your community? Who gives you strength, sharpens you?

____

____

How does having a community help you as a woman of faith? How does it help you in everyday life?

____

____

What is your weakest area of community? What is one step that you can take to build community in this part of your life?

Did the comment that "you get to choose your own community" surprise you? Why or why not?

Who is your family community? What are the challenges?

What is one positive thing about your family community?

What part can you play in a faith community? Is there anything that you do that causes friction in this community? Are you willing to take responsibility for your part?

Write down one thing that you can do today to find or strengthen the faith-based community that you need.

Lord, I need people with skin on. I need a family. Help me to take a risk and build community with others. Help me to find my place in a body of believers where I can express my faith and connect with others. Help me as I live independently, but also to link with others I call family. Thank you for the people that you will strategically place in my life, as I reach for community.

Love each other as if your life depended on it. Love makes up for practically anything. Be quick to give a meal to the hungry, a bed to the homeless—cheerfully. Be generous with the different things God gave you, passing them around so all get in on it: if words, let it be God's words; if help, let it be God's hearty help. That way, God's bright presence will be evident in everything through Jesus, and he'll get all the credit as the One mighty in everything—encores to the end of time. Oh, yes!

FROM 1 PETER 4

PART THREE: FAITH

More than just a religion

What a God w[illegible]ve! And how fortunate we are to have him, this F[illegible] of our Master Jesus! Because Jesus was raise[illegible] the dead, we've been given a brand-new life and have everything to live for.

FROM 1 PETER 1

Blog

What do I believe?

Current mood: contemplative

I grew up in church, but quit going to church sometime in my early 20s. I was confused by some of the people's lives and more importantly saw so many judgmental people that I didn't want to be a part of it anymore. I felt like I had to walk on eggshells, or like I needed to get saved again every day. But being away from church didn't mean I ran away from God. I spent time trying to figure out what I believe and why. It was time to quit believing just because my parents did.

I was drawn to a church in another city where I began to learn what it meant to be a believer. It is not about living a perfect life, walking on eggshells, being legalistic, or living someone else's convictions. It's about having a relationship with our awesome heavenly Father. It's about giving him our heart and drawing closer to him each day. The closer I get to God, the more I can hear him say what I should and shouldn't be doing. I think a lot of twentysomethings shy away from old-time religion because they are sick of hellfire and brimstone, they are sick of fake Christians, they are tired of not being able to live up to somebody else's standards and convictions, and perhaps they don't want to feel like a failure. They long for more. They long for true personal relationship, for intimacy with him.

For me, God was once all powerful and distant. Now I know him as my God, my best friend, my lover, my husband, my daddy, my provider, my healer, my obsession. Being held by him is absolutely amazing. In my opinion, this generation will come to know God as they are shown the love, mercy, goodness, and awesome supernatural power of our awesome father—in their lives. Then they will run to the Father!

Megan Mustain, twentysomething

SEVEN

What is my faith story?

MY NIECE CALLED ME AFTER returning home from a Young Life retreat.

"I get it now," she said.

The few times Kimberly and I had talked about faith, she referred to my spiritual experience with Christ as if it were a brand of religion. I tried to explain the difference. "I love God. My life is different because of the relationship. It's not just an affiliation with a church or a faith. It's so much deeper than that," I said.

She was respectful, but the distinction was blurry for her. As far as she could tell, her aunt was a religious woman; she was someone who called herself a Christian. She knew it affected every part of my life, but she didn't understand why it mattered. But Kimmy loved me, and if faith was part of who I was, she honored that. I prayed about it often. Kimberly is an amazing girl who was strong in spite of having faced some hard spots in life.

I desperately wanted to be able to share the fact that she was loved and cherished by a God that was real. That summer she met a friend involved in Young Life.* They invited her to a retreat, and it sounded like fun, so she went. One night one of the leaders shared that each of us has a choice: to believe that God exists. The next day Kimberly found a quiet place on the shore. As the waves

* For more information, see www.younglife.org.

slipped over her feet, she questioned God. For the first time she talked to him. And then something wonderful happened.

God became real to Kimberly.

That's when I received the phone call. "I understand now, Aunt Suzie. I really do."

For the first time religion had transitioned into relationship for Kimmy. I held the phone to my ear while tears slipped down my face.

I love stories. I remember my father telling the story of "The Three Billy Goats Gruff "when I was growing up. But I love other stories as well, those of lives changed by knowing Jesus Christ. I sit in awe many times, watching his story unfold in the lives of people who meet him for the first time. As in every story, there is a beginning, middle, and end. I get to see that person grasp who God is. I celebrate when they learn that they can turn to him, or when they pick themselves up after a particularly hard fall, with God's help. I love it when they discover his love, or what God can do with a willing heart.

Sometimes I sit and think about my own story. I go back to the beginning and I find the young girl, angry at God and the world. I see the young woman finding her way. I see the mother, the wife, the writer. I can't see the end of my story, but I know one thing. I know no matter the setting, the conflict, the plot, that there will always be one character that will weave its way through my story—and that is my God.

The story of faith

Entering a relationship with the God of the universe through Jesus Christ is never an idealistic or individualistic act,

> *though it is a personal decision. Instead, it is about a bigger purpose, a bigger story, a process, Christ's life automatically pours out of ours into others, like yeast in dough.*[1]
>
> JO KADLECEK, *DESPERATE WOMEN OF THE BIBLE*

A man named Nicodemus approached Jesus under cover of darkness. He was a religious man, respected in society. He followed rules and traditions and the seemingly impossible standards of his faith. His desire was to honor God. He was intrigued by Jesus, the guy from Galilee who was creating such controversy. Jesus said he was God's son. Nicodemus was curious about the man and his message that there was a simpler way to know God.[2] The discussion that night under the stars was an intelligent dialogue. Two men from two very different perspectives. Jesus told his new friend that he had come to be lifted up on a cross and to die so that Nicodemus and others could find life. He simplified the message of faith:

> This is how much God loved the world: He gave his Son, his one and only Son. And this is why: so that no one need be destroyed; by believing in him, anyone can have a whole and lasting life. God didn't go to all the trouble of sending his Son merely to point an accusing finger, telling the world how bad it was. He came to help, to put the world right again.[3]

This is the crux of Christianity, spoken plainly by the very one we say we believe in, so what does that mean to you and to me? It means that Christ came to earth so that you could know God. He came so that my life, your life, and those of all who desire to believe in him could be made right and whole by that love. Is this too simple? Perhaps the very simplicity of the gospel message is what confuses those who don't indulge in that love. How many times do we ourselves confuse this message because we load it down with our own interpretations, our own set of rules, our own hang-ups about our inadequacies and unworthiness? And likewise, how many times do we underestimate the power of following a Savior. I see his power when I read the Scripture that describes what happened upon his death. Upon his last breath there was "an earthquake, and rocks were split in pieces."[4] His resurrection three days later confirmed what he had shared all along. He was, indeed, the Son of God.

This fact is life changing as it influences your life story. What is faith? Is it relevant today? How does it impact you, and others around you? Let's look at three principles of faith:

1. Faith is meant to be personal.
2. Faith can withstand intellectual exploration.
3. Faith isn't about your goodness.

It's a personal journey

Faith is personal. It's not intended to be built solely upon the belief system of others. If your faith is built on sermons or a family tradition and you've never investigated it for yourself, it can disintegrate under pressure. Many twentysomethings are in universities of higher education to achieve degrees, but have invested little more than a seventh-grade education in faith. They know about religion. They know about tradition. They know about the message that Jesus Christ died upon a cross and came to life three days later to serve as the ultimate sacrifice. But those facts have not transformed the story of their life.

Faith changed me, and continues to define who I am, what I do, and where I am going. What is your story? Is it that you went to church your whole life, were a good girl, and strove to follow Christ in all that you do? Is your story like mine? Did you have no clue that God existed, only to find hope? Is it that you knew about God, made a lot of mistakes, and looked to him to find him again? These may be the synopses of your story, but let's go deeper. When did the story of faith impact you personally? When

did God become real to you? Unfortunately, there are people who go to church their whole life, but never find the depths and heights of *knowing* God.

Okay, Suzie, maybe this is me.

Christ came to earth, died upon a cross, and rose from the earth so that you and I could know him. We don't have to produce a formula to find that intimacy: *close your eyes, let me count to three, okay, now come to the altar.* I hate it when we make it a production. In the Bible, we find Christ walking along a shoreline finding men working in the cool air, scaling fish and folding their nets. "Want to join me?" he asked.

And they did. They put down everything to know the Messiah, even if they weren't sure that he was the promised Savior. That was the beginning of their faith story. They knew religion. They knew rules. They knew tradition, but from that day forward Jesus became real to them. They discovered the power of the Holy Spirit in a life open to direction. They realized that they were ordinary people, but that faith gave them purpose. They found that forgiveness came through him, rather than their own efforts. That when you *follow* Christ, instead of just knowing about him that faith integrates itself into every fiber of your being.

He calls you and me today, just like he did then. "Want to join me?" he asks. "Ready for the journey? Ready to discover what it means to know the God of the universe?" What does he want from you? A simple "yes." That's the beginning of your story. What unfolds from that moment forward is yet to be seen.

Just say yes.

Your doubts and questions don't intimidate God

There is room for doubt. There is room for questions. I continue to study and learn more about my Christian faith. I'm not afraid of intellectual growth in my faith. I want to understand and appreciate what and why I believe. 1 Corinthians 12 says this:

> Remember how you were when you didn't know God, led from one phony god to another, never knowing what you were doing, just doing it because everybody else did it? It's different in this life. God wants us to use our intelligence, to seek to understand as well as we can.

In the past few years I have gained an intense hunger for understanding. I read books to gain perspective on other cultures, mindsets, and even other religions so that I can talk with those who don't understand Christianity. But this only fuels my desire to know more about my own faith. I want to know what the Scriptures meant within the context and time that they were written. I want to know what great theologians believed. The surprising result of that hunger is that the more that I learn, the hungrier I am, and the more convinced I become. I don't want to base my beliefs upon what I hear. I want to experience it for myself. I want to read it for myself. The deeper I go into the heart of my faith, the simpler the message becomes as I scrape away all of the stuff that has been added on to the message since Christ walked the earth.

> "When I began walking this journey of awakening I was excited, but quickly I realized it was much harder than I ever thought it would be. I had to come face to face with the reality of my heart and my belief system. It was that phase of questioning. You know, you are away from your parents and wondering why you believe what you believe and if you've only believed it because you were conditioned to think that way. Did I only believe certain things about God because I was taught nothing more in my youth group? Did God really have a plan for my life? Could he provide financial miracles and healing in my heart? It was like God was calling my name. saying, 'Crystal, come deeper. I have so much more for you.' I was challenged and began to figure things out for myself."
>
> CRYSTAL HAHN, TWENTYSOMETHING

Though I respect many of the voices in my life, I do not

let them be the masters of my story. I love tradition. I explore doctrine because it teaches me to look at my faith in a relevant manner. I learn from theology and sermons, and from the advice from respected persons of faith. God places these mentors who know more than I do in my path. I gain knowledge from each of them, but they cannot be the foundation of my relationship with God; it must be personal.

Your faith story isn't about how good you are

Paul the apostle was once a religious man, burdened down with the complexities of rule-keeping. Listen to his impassioned plea to the church of Galatia:

> We know very well that we are not set right with God by rule-keeping but only through personal faith in Jesus Christ. How do we know? We tried it—and we had the best system of rules the world has ever seen! Convinced that no human being can please God by self-improvement, we believed in Jesus as the Messiah so that we might be set right before God by trusting in the Messiah, not by trying to be good.
>
> Have some of you noticed that we are not yet perfect? (No great surprise, right?) And are you ready to make the accusation that since people like me, who go through Christ in order to get things right with God, aren't perfectly virtuous, Christ must therefore be an accessory to sin? The accusation is frivolous. If I was "trying to be good," I would be rebuilding the same old barn that I tore down. I would be acting as a charlatan.
>
> What actually took place is this: I tried keeping rules and working my head off to please God, and it didn't work. So I quit being a "law man" so that I could be *God's* man.[5]

Paul brought the message down to one truth: This isn't about me! He was transformed. God became the energizer for the changes in his life. Rather than trying to become something in order to win God's favor, God changed him. He goes on to tell the Galatians the following:

> Christ's life showed me how, and enabled me to do it. I identified myself completely with him. Indeed, I have been crucified with Christ. My ego is no longer central. It is no longer important that I appear righteous before you or have your good opinion, and I am no longer driven to impress God. Christ lives in me. The life you see me living is not "mine," but it is lived by faith in the Son of God, who loved me and gave himself for me. I am not going to go back on that.
>
> Is it not clear to you that to go back to that old rule-keeping, peer-pleasing religion would be an abandonment of everything personal and free in my relationship with God? I refuse to do that, to repudiate God's grace. If a living relationship with God could come by rule-keeping, then Christ died unnecessarily.[6]

What about obedience? What about hearing the voice of God? Haven't I heard a thousand messages telling what I should or shouldn't do? When you allow him to develop what you already have right where you are, this is when the journey becomes tangible. It's not about how good you appear, because even that can become a trap. We come to see God through our goodness, rather than through his mercy. Is it about pleasing God or trusting God? We please God when we trust him.

And we learn how to trust him as we know him—his character, his presence, his Word.

I love to read the Bible. It enriches the way I see faith, the way I view others, as well as the way I view myself. It impacts my thinking. I learn to weigh decisions based upon the guidance I find in Scripture.

You and I become smaller as he becomes larger in our lives.

We spend alone time with God—not because of tradition, but because we find strength, direction, forgiveness, and peace in those moments.

At a conference I asked hundreds of twentysomethings to gather in a circle, and to talk honestly about the things that get in the way of alone time with God. The reasons were many. Then I shared the scripture in Matthew that promises that God knows what we need before we ask.[7] When we approach God, we find what we need. We don't have to pretend, or wear masks, or walk in with shame. He already knows, and he has what is needed.

> "I can't live off of someone else's faith. 'Sister so-and-so' can tell me what God did for her and I can rejoice with her and draw a modicum of faith from it. But until I dig through the trenches with God and come out on the other side with him, I won't really know how much he can truly do for me personally. It will all be just words or a good story told to me."
>
> Sarah Ballard, thirtysomething

I asked the women to share what they needed with each other. The needs were numerous, and great. Then I asked them to discuss what they might gain if they talked with God daily. For many, this was an *aha* moment.

God will see my weaknesses, won't he?

For others, it caused apprehension. Does the thought that God knows exactly where you are spiritually, emotionally, or physically bother you? Some perceive this aspect of the nature of God as intrusive. Why would I want God to know when I'm discouraged, or confused? Or when I mess up? Or when my motivations are less than what I hope for? Those are details in my story that I wish to erase. Except for the fact that this is when I need God the most.

Last October I stood behind a booth signing books. A woman had walked by the booth twice already. She approached a third time, and I introduced myself. I felt that I should pray with her, so I did. Later that day I strode through the massive hallways of the civic center. Women sat in clusters on the floor, eating their lunch, comparing notes, laughing. As I stepped over feet and legs, a pair of off-white heels caught my eye. I stopped, knelt down, and looked into the eyes of the person that belonged to the shoes.

> "In my pursuit of becoming the woman I am supposed to be, I have had to let God take all the bad and replace it with good. The roots of these things are sometimes so deep and it really hurts as God begins to destroy them. And this process for me is taking way too long. I know I am not anywhere near complete. But even though this process is extremely painful I want it to continue. I want him to take all my mistakes, my own plans and replace them with his awesome plan."
>
> Megan Mustain, twentysomething

Something about those shoes commanded me to slow down long enough to notice the person wearing them. It was the woman who had stopped by my booth earlier. My personal assistant stood patiently by, and I sensed her desire to get me to the next stop before the women filled the room. I reached down and tweaked the toe of the woman's shoe. "Hey," I said, and that was it. I looked at her and smiled. I stood, and went on to my next workshop. I felt a little silly, but this is what I didn't know.

I didn't know that she burst into tears after I left.

I didn't know that she didn't want to be at the conference.

I didn't know that she was discouraged and felt alone in a crowd of 2000 women.

I didn't know that she had just asked God to show her that he knew she existed.

Sometimes God stops the world on its axis for a moment to reach down and give one of his daughters a gentle kiss—just to let her know that he's there. He saw her that day. I've my own moments of doubt or insecurity, and pushed everything to the side just to get alone with God, and found him waiting just for me. God sees you and me, and that can be a beautiful revelation.

Do you long to see him as well? It's not complicated. Jesus

said, "Here's what I want you to do: Find a quiet, secluded place so you won't be tempted to role-play before God. Just be there as simply and honestly as you can manage. The focus will shift from you to God, and you will begin to sense his grace."[8] If you desire to include him in your story, then will you consider halting the production of your own story long enough to seek him? My alone place is a small dock overlooking a pond beside my house. You might live in a high-rise apartment in a large city, or with two children tugging at your legs in a suburban home. Your alone place will not look like mine, but when we shut out the world, if only for a few moments each day, there's an opportunity to connect with God in a one-on-one.

Listen to the story of your life

God is already aware of what is going on in your life, so why not find encouragement, strength, maturity, and peace, but also new paragraphs, exclamation points, question marks, and ellipses written in that day's narrative? Keri Wyatt Kent, author of *Listen,* says, "Your accomplishments, your struggles, and your desires all become important elements in your story."[9]

My friend, Keri, is an energetic, tall 40-something woman who walks fast and talks with passion. She seems like the type of woman who might struggle to slow down. Keri began her career as a newspaper reporter, then branched out to become an author, and is now a Bible teacher. When I read her books *(Breathe; Listen;* and *Oxygen),* I was instantly drawn to the deep spiritual insights within the pages.

Though she is an energetic busy person, underneath she is calm and deep. Keri believes that sometimes life becomes so hectic that we forget to listen to the story of our lives.

> We are too busy, too hurried. Multi-tasking gets in the way of listening. If we want to listen to a friend, we turn off the cell phone, we sit down and look them in the eye.

> We give them our attention because we refuse to give it to other things, for that moment. Listening communicates love. So it's the same with God. If we say we love God but we don't ever just turn off all our noise (phone, iPod, and so on) and sit and be with him, then it's a pretty shallow love.[10]

Are you listening? Have you put aside all the hype and noise and clutter of opinion to really tune in to him? Have you slowed down long enough to get alone with God, to rediscover his presence in the story of your life?

> "We are bombarded with so much information, a lot of it advertising or spam. Everyone seems to be selling something, and the tendency is to block it out or turn it off."
>
> KATIE HART, TWENTYSOMETHING

It is not only the busyness of our lives that gets in the way of discovering our story, but sometimes fear can be a culprit. Keri believes that there's a reason why one of the most-often-repeated commandments in the Bible is this: Do not be afraid.

> Sometimes we don't listen, both to other people or to God, because we're afraid. Afraid they might say something that would make us uncomfortable or ask for more than we're willing to give. Afraid we'll say the wrong thing and the other person or God will bail on the relationship. Afraid of awkward silence. I think we're also afraid that God will point out all our faults. But I think that God always speaks with the voice of love, and never with the voice of shame.[11]

Fear is a scarecrow

Perhaps fear is best described by Craig Groeschel, in *Confessions of a Pastor.* Fear is a scarecrow, he says:

> What harm can a scarecrow do? We scarecrow constructors know that the answer is "none," but the birds

> don't know that...If those blackbirds ever figured out our strategy, they'd realize that a scarecrow is actually a tip-off to the location of the best corn![12]

Possibly, your fears are an indicator of what God believes you can be, can do, and can discover if you only allowed him to write the next scene. Though I am confident in many ways, I face fear. Even as I write this book, I am concerned that I won't complete my deadline on time. I worry that I have overextended my boundaries. Though I have amazing conversations about life and faith with twentysomethings, I wonder who I think that I am to speak to you—a person I've never met, and yet I know God has placed this project on my heart.

> "Faith is impractical. Faith often tells me to do the opposite of what makes sense. Faith tells me to trust God, even when I don't feel his trustworthiness."
>
> B.J. Hamrick, twentysomething

Those are the times that I refocus and listen once more to the creator of my story. Sometimes that means that I put it all down for a moment, and carefully make sure that that I'm doing what I should (instead of just trying to publish another book or accept another opportunity because it seems like the right thing to do). Or I invite him into the process, letting him take me where I should go. Though I may not know you, God does, and thus he becomes the perfect partner in your work or ministry.

When I wrote my last book, *The Mom I Want to Be,* I set the project aside 15 or 20 times in the course of writing it. *What if the story of my painful past helps others, but hurts my mom? Should I really reveal the details of abuse? Should I be this honest?* When the book was released, my mother's story touched the lives of many and she gained a voice. The world saw the ugliness of the past, but they also saw a miracle. Her story of brokenness and subsequent emotional healing touched lives. Together, we found the "best corn."

Fear hid the fact that thousands of women have experienced dysfunction, and seek answers to issues such as forgiveness, breaking down walls, restoring relationships, and giving their children something greater. The very things I feared—*God, is this too honest, too real?*—was exactly what these women sought. God knew that, even when I did not. He knew their story. He allowed my story, and that of my mother, to help them find their way to the next chapter.

Have you ever thought of your life as a story? What chapter are you on right now?

____

____

If the story of faith is a simple message, then why does it seem so complex?

____

____

Is it possible that fear is the obstacle to discovering something greater in your story? Is it fear of others, fear that you don't measure up, or fear that you might be asked to do something for which you feel unprepared? Explain this.

____

____

Faith is first personal. What might get in the way of that personal relationship?

____

____

Do you ever struggle to listen? Why?

____

____

If you could share one thing with God that was so real and raw that you've not shared it with anyone, what would it be? Rather than write it down, will you consider getting alone with God right now and inviting him to help you with this? Share your experience.

Jesus, today I realized that you are writing the story of my life. You see the chapter I am on right now. You see where I am. But you also see the beginning and the possibilities of what can be. I invite you into the story of my life. I strap on faith and fearlessness as you take me places I don't see yet. Thank you for writing my story, and that the story of your life is inscribed upon my heart.

They suddenly recognize that God is a living, personal presence, not a piece of chiseled stone. And when God is personally present, a living Spirit, that old, constricting legislation is recognized as obsolete. We're free of it! All of us! Nothing between us and God, our faces shining with the brightness of his face. And so we are transfigured much like the Messiah, our lives gradually becoming brighter and more beautiful as God enters our lives and we become like him.

FROM 2 CORINTHIANS 3

So close, but so far away

Current mood: peaceful

Do you ever feel like you are so close to having something in your grasp, but then you can't seem to find the footing to take hold? I have been finding myself in this state quite often it seems. One day I will feel an overwhelming sense of God and his desires for me, then the next day somehow a whirlwind of "who am I?" sets in. I am trapped in a state of comparison. I wish I were more like her; I wish I could do this, if only I had this. In this state, I find my mind constantly fighting confusion and distraction. Then, almost simultaneously I find myself slipping in and out of apathy. There is a pull deep inside to be focused, determined, disciplined, to see and reach the goals before me. There seems to be something keeping me from it, an invisible wall—or is that wall me?

At this point, I want to throw up my hands and scream, but then when I am at the peak of frustration, I am suddenly soothed with a quiet peace and a beautiful voice saying, *Rest in me.* Rest. What a crazy thought in a time like this, but so ironically, in the middle of my desperate search to understand, I find truth in the fact that I cannot conjure up this walk. I cannot figure it all out.

I feel like I should have the answers and that by now in my "Christian walk" I should have it somewhat mastered. I am figuring out that I am at rest most, when I accept I am weak. There is such power in this. A power that I don't want to admit, but once I say it, a release takes place and the obvious need for a Savior consumes my soul.

I focus on what lies within my grasp—just on the other side. In the past, I relied on my abilities and strengths to have a sense of direction and purpose, now I find freedom in my fears, doubts, and confusions. I am weak; I might fail, but I can fall and land in my Father's arms and rest. It's a true rest because I abandon my preconceived ideas and take hold of Jesus who shatters my perceptions and takes me to the other side.

Crystal Hahn, twentysomething

EIGHT

They say I'm called...to what?

I KNELT AT THE FRONT of the church alone.

"What should I be doing?" I asked. My question was sincere, my heart troubled. I left my job two years earlier to pursue what I thought was my calling—to pursue what I thought I was made to do. Was it my writing? Was it motherhood? Was it speaking? I wrestled with this simple word laden with such distinction—my *call.*

"Tell me, God. Tell me what I need to do."

When I left my career track I went home to spend time with my children, and to pursue my love of writing. I didn't realize how much my job had defined me until the first paycheck failed to show, or the day that I traded my career clothing for jeans and a T-shirt. I loved being home, but I was adapting to a different lifestyle. I was used to well-laid plans. In the corporate world, if I worked hard and continued to learn about the business, I could rise in the company. It wasn't an overnight process, but there was at least a road map to success.

Shifting to freelance writing and ministry crumpled the map and threw it out the window.

I worked in my makeshift home office. I pursued prospective assignments. I struggled with the fact that *freelance* meant you might get paid and you might not, or that you could work hard, send an invoice, and receive a meager paycheck two months later.

In the corporate world there were plenty of pats on the back from colleagues, or at least in the form of a Christmas bonus!

In spite of these challenges, I wanted to impact the world one word at a time.

As I sat quietly, I saw a foot swinging. I wiped my eyes.

"Hey, buddy—sorry I didn't see you." I smiled at Brandon and Laney. Laney, 5 years old, chewed her gum with gusto. Brandon, who was 13, sat patiently. He had long, dark blond hair. He wore a backwards ponytail that hung between his eyes like a garden snake.

"Can we have a ride home?"

"Absolutely," I said. "Anyone hungry?"

I knew they would be. Things were tough in their home. Mom was pregnant and also sick with Hepatitis C. Dad was in jail for selling drugs. They lived in a part of town that made me shudder when I dropped them off after church services—not because of the small homes or the ramshackle streets, but because of the men who stood in clusters after dark. It was a place where people rented month to month, and often landlords removed the doors from the hinges, regardless of the weather or danger, to make renters leave when they didn't pay. There were drug deals in the streets. And there were the stories that Laney shared casually—tales that would make many adults afraid, though she spoke of them in everyday terms. I wrapped my arms around the two children, I felt Brandon's fierce hug, and Laney's simple trust as she grabbed my hand.

And suddenly I saw the answer to my question. It was as clear as if it had been plastered on a billboard on a busy city street.

Brandon and Laney were my calling. At least, for that day. They were my special task. I didn't need a road map. I didn't need to have God spell it out for me. My calling is to live as a woman of faith every day. That day's special mission might be to love my friends or text message a note of encouragement. It might be to hug my kids, or encourage my husband. It might be to write an

article that will help someone I don't know, but who God knows on a first-name basis. It might be to sing to God while I clean the bathroom or wash my car, or to hold my tongue when someone made me angry.

It was all of those things.

But for that moment, my calling was to take Brandon and Laney to Burger King and buy them a burger and fries.

Laney and Brandon's mother moved to a different city to be closer to family, and to be able to visit her husband in the jail. A few years passed, and I didn't hear anything, and soon they were a distant, sweet memory. One day I walked into a large warehouse store in Tulsa. I felt a whoosh of air and strong arms wrapped around me from behind, nearly picking me up off of the cement floor.

"Mama Suzie!"

It was Brandon. He was nearly 19. He worked at the store and lived at his grandmother's home. For the next few moments we caught up. He took me around and introduced me to a few co-workers, explaining who I was and telling them with pride that I was an author.

"How are Laney and your mom?" I asked. "And your dad?"

His dad had become a Christian in prison and the transformation was real. He had been released from jail and for the past three years was active in a small church. Brandon's mom was in remission, her health better now that she wasn't carrying the load alone. She was also able to go back to her profession, which was nursing.

Things weren't perfect for Brandon, but they were better, much better than they were when he was the angry middle school student I first met.

"And you?" I asked. "How are you?"

He told me that he was working to restore an older car, and that he hoped to go to trade school and become a mechanic. He paused, wiping a strand of hair off of his face. "I've never forgotten you. My whole family hasn't forgotten you, and for a long time your picture was on the refrigerator at my mom's house."

I was stunned. The reality is that what I offered Brandon and Laney was so small compared to the need. Rides home. Hugs. A few cheeseburgers. Sometimes I produced very small things just to help for the moment, but they faced challenges that seemed insurmountable at times. I often felt overwhelmed by what I could not do.

But Brandon saw it differently. He viewed it through the eyes of a person who learned that God cared because he was hungry, and someone fed him.

Divine discontentment

> *He only stirs us when he wants to change us.*
> *He only makes us feel uneasy with where we are so we're willing to do whatever it takes to get where he is.*[1]
>
> Joanna Weaver, fortysomething author of *Having a Mary Spirit*

Have you ever felt discontentment? There are many sources for this feeling, but we often assume the root of discontentment to be disappointment—in ourselves, or perhaps even from God. *I'm not doing enough. I'm not where I should be. Is God dissatisfied with me?* It's a form of self-condemnation that very rarely produces positive change, and it's far from scriptural. It doesn't launch you into action or help you find the answers to the questions you are asking. What would happen if you allowed that divine discontentment to move you, instead of mire you? To be expectant instead of unenthusiastic? To teach you instead of thwart you?

I have faced seasons of discontent. Times that I wanted so badly to do something, anything, to feel as if I were moving forward, that I overlooked the significance of what was occurring at the moment. That's what God was showing me through Brandon and Laney. I had failed to see the smaller picture. We're trained—encouraged, pushed—to see the big picture, but I believe that one day we'll have an opportunity to view our lives in full spectrum and that we'll be surprised at the things that really matter. Or perhaps how the small things pieced together to create a mosaic of significance.

God is working in and through your life right where you are today. Your calling isn't a PowerPoint slide chart, but rather a moment-to-moment unfolding of events as you live as a biblical woman—at home, at work, at school, when you're alone or in the crowd, when life is good or it is crappy. No matter where you are or where you're going.

In *My Life with the Saints,* James Martin writes,

> While I'm always called to grow, God only asks that I be myself, no matter what the situation. So when I'm listening to a friend tell me his problems, or hearing someone's confession, or standing before a homeless man in the street, I don't have to say what would Peter or Francis or Therese or John XXIII do. Certainly they are models of Christian action for me. But God has not placed them in this particular situation.[2]

These saints left a lasting impression, but it is not one event or moment that made them icons, but rather a life of cumulative actions that resulted in greatness. Perhaps there were moments of weakness, or indecision. Perhaps one or all of them wondered if their life mattered. Yet they made a difference right where they were, and upon the people around them.

As you move toward your goals in your career, or move forward with your relationships, or as you attempt to uncover your overarching purpose, consider three principles to help you understand your "calling":

1. Your daily call affects the roles that you play, and the career or ministries that you choose.
2. You won't always see the entire picture.
3. Your daily call helps you grow in grace and strength.

The colors of your life

My mother is an artist. She sees things in a different light than I do. When she takes a picture, she sees the light playing on the outskirts. She sees the shadows. She sees color as multidimensional. Red and green are beautiful side by side, but together they create a rich green hue.

When you live your calling daily, it adds new colors to all the roles that you play. Perhaps in your career, you begin to view your co-workers or the boss from Hades as loved by God, and perhaps discover that the mission field God has "called" you to for now are the people around you. It's not living perfectly, or trying to be something that you are not, but rather being open to the opportunities around you today.

As a student, you might feel alone in your faith. What is your calling? Is it the student living in the apartment next door? Is it to live a life of consistent faith no matter where you are, or who you are with? Is it to pray for a friend whose heart is broken? Is it to live with convictions in an environment where convictions might be questioned?

As a young mom, you are called to live out your faith. Rather than seeing diapers and long nights without sleep, you also see the impact that you have upon young, tender lives, and their impact upon your life. You live your calling in the moment. You show God's love when you hold your child and they feel safe. You look for God moments when your child points out a beautiful sky and

believes that he painted it just for her. You turn to God when the sheer day-to-day responsibilities are overwhelming.

When you refocus to see those opportunities and moments as your calling, rather than completely focusing on the end destination, each of the experiences, battles, new relationships, and moments all contain the ability to teach you. I'm not saying that you don't need a general road map, but the individual experiences and moments help you become better equipped, so that when you approach the desired destination you're ready. Too often, people acquire their dreams far before they are prepared to handle them. In every area—whether it's privilege, money, fame, relationships, ministry, or your career—there are complexities that arrive with dreams. We must learn to deal with people with grace or wisdom. We must grasp that money is a tool, and that power is fleeting and often troublesome, that there are people all around us who may not seem influential, but who can be friends or teachers. Or recognize those who seem to have great influence, but whose power upon our lives is far from healthy.

If you live in the big picture 100 percent of the time, you might miss these very important life lessons, arriving at the destination with external success, but little internal insight. This is the secret I discovered when I began to live my calling daily: All the small things add up!

Event/person/circumstance	*Cost*	*Life lesson*
Laney and Brandon	Time	Compassion
Dealing with difficult person	Self-control	Patience
Cancer	My well-laid plans	Trust

I could write an entire book on the thousands of daily events that have transpired in the past 47 years. Most of them were not included in my overall plan, but when I evaluate them, I find the impact upon my life to be priceless.

What about you? Consider your life right now. As you went

through your day today, did you notice the people that crossed your path? Reflect upon your circumstances. Do they rob you of the ability to see beyond them? Take a moment to consider the small brushstrokes in your day and how the rich hues add to the picture of your life.

Sometimes I get off track when I see my calling in a too-large frame. I try to write enough books, or speak at enough conferences, all with a heart to minister, but it's painted in strokes that are too broad. It is the feathery touches that make the portrait complete, like Brandon's smile or Laney's hand in mine.

Behind the scenes

As a writer I rarely hear the response to my articles or books, unless it is negative. I receive a few e-mails. I read the yearly sales report. I read reviews on Amazon.com, but I very rarely receive affirmation. I knew this when I began this profession, but it's much different than when I worked in the "real world." There were instant results. If I wrote a great presentation I received a pat on the back. There were annual reviews. If I worked hard, I received a promotion and a title and cold, hard cash. As a writer, it would be easy to drive myself to frustration trying to figure out what people think. To remain in this business, you learn to trust that God is big enough to do the work behind the scenes. But every once in a while, you get a glimpse.

This past summer I taught at a writer's conference and was approached after class by a woman. "You're T. Suzanne Eller," she said. "You wrote an article about self-injury."

I nodded, remembering how difficult this particular article was to place. Cutting is a rising phenomenon among teens, so I interviewed several experts in the field, as well as teens who had overcome self-injury. I presented the information to a couple of magazines with which I had a working relationship, but was rejected, saying "not a great fit." They didn't care for the topic, and felt that it wasn't an issue that many people were concerned with.

However, I realized that it was a perfect fit. I met young girls (and a few teen guys) on a weekly basis who were cutting. I needed the facts for myself if I were to minister effectively, but also felt that parents could use information that was compassionate, practical, spiritual, and that would reveal the underlying problems with self-injury. It took months to finally find a faith-based magazine to accept the article, and nearly a year of effort netted a whopping $400 paycheck.

The woman interrupted my thoughts to continue her story. She teared up. "Your article came at just the right time." Then she shared her story.

Her brother worked overseas as a missionary and he and his wife discovered that their teen was self-injuring. As a family they were devastated, and they desperately sought resources to help their daughter. The advice that they received from well-meaning friends only made matters spiral. Finally, they considered a number of options, and one of those was leaving the mission field to seek professional help for their family.

That week the woman received her favorite Christian magazine in the mail and was shocked to find an article on self-injury with practical help, but also a list of experts to consult. She immediately made a copy of the article and faxed it to her brother.

"It was just what they needed," she said. "That article helped them to know what to do. They knew how to deal with the real problem instead of concentrating on the self-injury only. Their daughter is doing great; she's recovered and the family now knows what to look for, and how to deal with the problem if it ever arises. Your article really opened up communication between my brother and his daughter. She knows that she can come to him if she feels overwhelmed, or tempted to cut." She paused. "I can't believe that I've met you. I've wanted to thank you."

It was an accident that I ran into this woman, but then again, maybe it was not. That's another thing that I've learned when I live my calling daily. Sometimes accidents are actually moments where you get a glimpse of how God works behind the scenes.

This was what was on my mind as I battled to publish that article. *Will anyone publish this article? How can I explain that this is an important topic? If I worked in the corporate world, I would have made thousands of dollars instead of pennies on the hour. I know that self-injury is impacting our Christian teens too—can we please talk about it?*

Small picture. Small picture. Small picture.

Consider with me this scenario: A family trusted God enough to leave extended family and familiarity to make a new life. Their work touched the lives of others. Thousands of miles away, a writer struggled to place an article, wondering if it would ever find a home. At just the right time, the article emerged to help the missionary family. The missionary's sister ran into the writer at a conference, and shared her story, affirming the writers' passion and fueling her desire to continue to write.

Big picture.

What a beautiful cycle. What beautiful timing.

I believe that one day we will be astounded at how a word of encouragement, or a card sent at the right time, or how an act of patience or kindness ignited a series of events that unfolded without our knowledge; or how that our failures are actually successes. One of my favorite movies is *Pay It Forward*. In it, eleven-year-old Trevor McKinney is challenged by his Social Studies teacher to come up with a plan to change the world. Most of the students in the class don't take the assignment seriously, but Trevor does, creating the Pay It Forward theory: If one person performs three selfless acts, and each of the benefactors do the same (paying it forward), it would spawn a movement of selfless acts that could change the world.

> "Love is really what we are all looking for."
>
> JAMIE SCHNEIDER, TWENTYSOMETHING

McKinney tries with three people—a homeless man, his mother, and his social-studies teacher—and it appears that all three fail. The homeless man goes back to his drugs. His mother

goes back into an abusive relationship. His teacher remains a loner. McKinney confesses that his efforts to create Pay It Forward were in vain, until a once-jaded reporter finds him and shares that McKinney's selfless actions started a ripple effect that spawned a movement spanning across the nation.

Though McKinney, and his mother and teacher, eventually saw the fruits of one boy's actions, in real life we very rarely see beyond the obvious. It's why discouragement sets in, and we wonder if what we are doing is really making a difference, or if we should be doing something grander or more visible. If my calling is to live my faith daily, then there is not only a plan for me, but God can take my daily life and create something far greater than I can see.

Where do I start?

What if I miss my calling? How can I recognize these special moments? Do you realize how busy I am? Who's paying attention to what I'm saying or doing anyway?

Have you ever traveled with someone who strapped everyone in the car, and then drove like a madman—refusing to stop no matter how attractive a site, no matter how badly someone needed to go to the bathroom, staring at the map, but forgetting to enjoy the trip? I have, and I refuse to ever do so again. I won't do it on a road trip, and I don't believe that we're meant to approach life that way either. I don't have to frantically look for ways to live out my faith.

All I need to do is to be aware that these moments occur, and recognize them when they happen, and then respond. You daily ask the Holy Spirit to help you become attuned to the needs around you, for you are promised that the Holy Spirit will make "everything plain."[3] What is made plain is the need or the opportunity; what you might not see is how far-reaching the results might be.

In the book of Esther, we find a young Jewish woman whose uncle worked for the king as a scribe. King Xerxes threw a six-month long party and his wife, the queen, refused to show up when he asked her to perform an impromptu fashion show for his friends. A few of his counselors took advantage of the king's bad temper, and advised him to banish the queen. When his anger cooled, he regretted his actions and was lonely, but his word was law, so his servants advised him to find a new queen.

Mordecai, the king's scribe, brought his beautiful niece Esther to the palace, and she won over the heart of the king, and became the new queen. While this might sound like a complicated love story, Esther became a pivotal player in a much larger scene. One of the king's highest ranking officials, Haman, was plotting to kill all of the Jews in the nation. He was a man hungry for power, and the king was blind to this man's evil heart. Haman laid out a plan and the king consented, unaware of the far-reaching effect, or even that his wife was a Jew.

That night Mordecai approached his niece, asking her to talk with her husband, the king. She was fearful, because in that day if you approached the king (even if you were the queen) without permission he could have you killed. She was afraid, but Mordecai reminded her that this moment was pivotal. He said, "Maybe you were made queen for just such a time as this."[4] She didn't have to look for ways to live out her faith; they came to her. She simply needed to be aware of the moment, and that she was the woman of the hour.

Henry T. Blackaby, in *Called and Accountable,* says, "In the entire process, God takes the initiative to come to his people and to let them know what he is doing or about to do." Blackaby lists several ordinary individuals from the Bible who went on to become extraordinary, saying, "God encountered each person right in the middle of their daily routine, brought them to himself, and then used them to accomplish his work."[5]

Where do you begin? First, be available. Slow down long

enough to hear the quiet tug on the inside of you that says, "Do you see that?" Invite God to be a part of your day from the moment that you wake up. Ask him to speak to your heart, to help you to see others as he does.

Do you want to try it right now? What is God speaking to your heart as you read this? Look around you. What have you failed to notice that is around you, blending into the background as you whisk by? What is beautiful? What might you see differently if you paused, if only for a moment?

Living your call daily creates a woman of grace and strength

I met Joanna Weaver in Denver, Colorado. Her book, *Having a Mary Heart in a Martha World,* was (and continues to be) a bestseller, topping out the charts for nearly six years. She's a mom to three and a pastor's wife, living in Montana. Those were the facts I gleaned from the back of her book, but when I met her in person I discovered a gentle, fun, and faith-filled women. She exuded grace, and greeted me with a warm smile. As we talked, I felt I'd made an instant friend.

Joanna's story is not typical in the fast track to success. After her book hit the bestseller list, readers eagerly awaited a sequel. In her next book, *Having a Mary Spirit,* Joanna describes what happened instead. She sensed she needed a break and scheduled a six-month hiatus. Writing the first book while in full-time ministry and being a mom and wife had left her depleted, and she wanted time to refuel. Six months turned into six years. She watched her children grow up, then God surprised her with a child just as she turned 40. When the church she and her husband serve began a new building program, she discovered a vision and passion she hadn't felt in a long time.

Joanna found herself slipping back into her former Martha busy mode, running at full tilt. She went to bed thinking about the building project, lining up the numerous details that needed to be completed the next day. She was excited to be doing something for her church and for God, and kept up the frenzied pace. Her husband warned her she was going to burn out if she didn't slow down, but she continued. She writes about that time:

> I brushed away John's concerns. Sure, this was a crazy time, I told myself. Getting a ball rolling takes a lot of effort. I'd slow down later...I slowed down, all right. Brick walls have that effect on people...Every option I came up with was discarded and, to be honest, my insistence began to wear on people. Finally, I had to admit that God must have other things in mind.[6]

She describes this time as "running ahead of God." I relate to that. I want things to happen—now! I might be described as patient, but I wrestle with it on a daily basis. I want what I want today, and am frustrated when it seems that my dreams are on time delay. It's not about material things; it's about my dreams. It's what I inadvertently describe as my calling.

However, if my real passion is to live out my faith daily, then I discover that God isn't as concerned with my dreams as he is with the dreamer. He looks beneath the surface to see my attitude, my motivations, my methods—and perhaps reveals the things I least want to see about myself. But rather than being a harsh act, it is an act of grace on God's part. He gives me the help I need to discover greater heights and depths within me. In Romans 8, we are encouraged to allow the Holy Spirit to join us on this journey:

> Those who think they can do it on their own end up obsessed with measuring their own moral muscle but never get around to exercising it in real life. Those who trust God's action in them find that God's Spirit is in them—living and breathing God! Obsession with self in these matters is a dead end; attention to God leads us out into the open, into a spacious, free life. Focusing on the self is the opposite of focusing on God. Anyone completely absorbed in self ignores God, ends up thinking more about

> self than God. That person ignores who God is and what he is doing. And God isn't pleased at being ignored.
>
> But if God himself has taken up residence in your life, you can hardly be thinking more of yourself than of him. Anyone, of course, who has not welcomed this invisible but clearly present God, the Spirit of Christ, won't know what we're talking about. But for you who welcome him, in whom he dwells—even though you still experience all the limitations of sin—you yourself experience life on God's terms.

Living my calling daily means I become vulnerable, opening every door of my life to allow the Holy Spirit to gently do a walk-through. *Look in this place, Suzie. There is pride. It's not arrogance, but it won't benefit you where I'm taking you, and the effect upon others could be harmful. Will you take a look at this? See it for what it is, and then let's extract this from your being. Look here, Suz. You're angry at this person. She hurt one of your loved ones. No one knows, but I see it. What do you wish for me to do with this hidden resentment?*

Daily interaction helps me to stay authentic in my walk. It produces humility—the ability to be real about who I am, and who I am not, as I trust God. The result is spiritual maturity, and what the Bible calls, in Galatians 5, the fruit of the Spirit: love, joy, peace, patience, kindness, goodness, gentleness, self-control, and faithfulness. When Joanna Weaver placed everything down once again, she found contentment. And God opened the right doors at the right time for this grace-filled woman. She writes,

> My deepest fear is waking up twenty years from now still the same woman I am today. With the same annoying habits and petty attitudes; with the same besetting sins and false beliefs. I can't imagine anything more terrible than getting to the end of my life only to discover that God had so much more in mind for me—more freedom, more joy, more peace, more true effectiveness. And I had missed it all, simply because I refused to change.[7]

This is perhaps the best-kept secret of all. When we live our calling daily, God is the one who opens the doors, or shuts them, at the right time. We pray, we plan, we dream and we hope. We prepare. But we also keep in mind that God may have something far greater in mind than we ourselves can construct. As I look back, I see my hopes marching alongside God's plans for me. I see the detours that I took, the times I felt as if I were alone, the times I battled circumstances, or felt immersed in the smaller details of my existence. Recently in a conversation with a friend, my husband said, "When Suzie was sick with cancer, she didn't change. God was important in her life the day before she was sick, and he remained important the day after."

> "Faith is as easy as trusting, but most of the time that is the hardest thing about faith! I want to do things my way and in my timing. I have a really hard time putting my faith in him and letting him do what he has planned. I want things now and my way, but then I'm reminded that it's not my way and it's not my timing. It's his. Faith is something that I struggle with every day, giving up myself, my timing, my wants and desires, and letting God take over. Trusting in every aspect of my life and letting God take control."
>
> MICHELLE PLUNKETT, TWENTYSOMETHING

I am humbled by that word picture, but I see it in a different light. My life changes moment by moment, but God is unchanging. If I tap into that strong rock and live my faith daily, then his strength becomes mine. He reveals truth to me when I cannot see because of the darkness of my feelings.

And his wisdom guides me, leading me places I might not find otherwise.

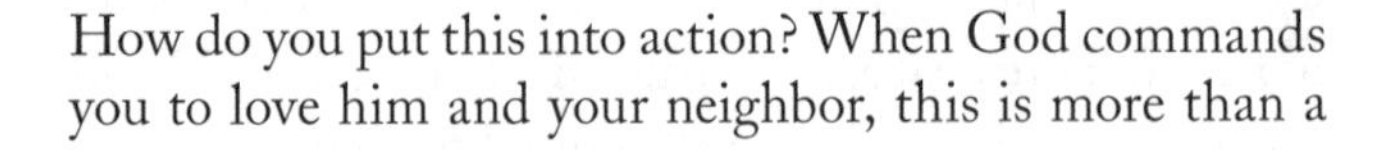

How do you put this into action? When God commands you to love him and your neighbor, this is more than a

commandment. In a sense, it is a promise that the Holy Spirit will produce that love within you. There are practical steps you can take to allow him to do this. Think of someone whom you should genuinely love, but don't. Now ask God to give you a great love for that person. Then ask him to show you how you can show that love to him or her. Share your experience.

Define the word *calling* as described in this chapter. Is this a different perspective for you?

Do you ever worry too much about the bigger picture, but fail to see the small picture?

Is it possible that God's plans are different than yours? What would you do if you discovered this to be true?

Are you open to allowing God to change you from the inside out? Does this make you feel vulnerable? Why or why not?

How does living your calling daily affect the various roles that you play in life (student, daughter, career woman, wife, girlfriend, citizen...)?

Father, I am called to live out my faith every day. Jesus is my example. He saw people through eyes of eternity. Even in his suffering, he reached out to others. I live in a busy world, God, and not only do I sometimes miss the beauty of all that is around me, but I strive and work to make things happen in my life. I know that you have a plan for my life. I want to be a dreamer. I want to believe that I can play a part. But I also want you to help me to see my calling in the moments of my life.

Open my eyes, God.

Work from the heart for your real Master, for God, confident that you'll get paid in full when you come into your inheritance. Keep in mind always that the ultimate Master you're serving is Christ.

FROM COLOSSIANS 3

Blog

It's hard to give so much

Current mood: reflective

How many times have I thought the same thing? *Hey, do I need to give everything?* This is something that God deals with me every day, because honestly, I am naturally a selfish person. First it was with money. It wasn't real hard to tithe until we started making more money. Why is it the more God gives us the harder it is to give back to him? But we found out that by staying faithful in that area, we have never gone without.

Now I sometimes get stingy with my time. When God calls me to do something I groan and get all in a funk when I should just get up and do it, and be happy that God called me to do something. I also struggle in spending time with him every day. I get so distracted with my everyday life that I forget to read my Bible or pray. Then by the end of the day I'm usually exhausted.

I've been really praying for help with this because it's so important.

Shawna Glass, twentysomething

NINE

Gucci or giving?

"READY TO WRITE THE CHECK, SUZ?" Richard asked.

I nodded, but inside I was shaking my head. No, I wasn't ready to write the check. Weren't we faithful to pay 10 percent of our income to our local church? Hadn't I bought candy bars I didn't need to eat, and candles and expensive trinkets I didn't want to use, in order to support the latest school fund-raiser? Everywhere I turned it seemed like a hand was out. It's not that I'm tightfisted, but I had added up all the money going out and it seemed that all that was left was bills.

I didn't want a luxury car or a huge home. I didn't want expensive clothing.

I just wanted a few extra bucks to put in my pocket and call it my own.

The check we'd received was a bonus. Money we didn't expect. Taxes had taken nearly half before we ever cashed it. Now we were going to give away a large part of what was left.

There are a thousand things I could do with this money.

The thought interrupted me as I wrote the check. I closed my eyes. This was a sum we had agreed together to pay toward a good cause. But my heart wasn't in it. Not for one second.

Cheerful giver? If I'm honest, not really.

I sat in a small room in a refugee camp in Vienna, Austria. There were families from all over the world represented in the camp. As we spoke, I talked in English. It was translated to German, then to Farsi, and around the room it went as one person spoke their language to the next, who translated in yet another tongue. Languages intermingled like couples at a dance. But the stories were the same. Different characters. Different wars or disruptions. Different families with different cultures. But all of them sharing stories of atrocities performed by their fellow man.

Several had lost family members. All of them had lost possessions. One woman was skinny with sunken cheeks. She showed me a picture of a woman. The person in the photo was portly but beautiful. Her hair was glossy black. Her clothing was exquisite. She sat on a carved chair, surrounded by heirloom furniture. A rich tapestry hung in the background. "Do you recognize this person?" she asked.

I shook my head no.

She laughed, hiding her smile behind her hand. "It is me," she said. "This was my home. This was me!"

It was hard to believe that this person once wore those clothes or lived in comfort. The room we stood in was made of cinderblocks, dorm-style, with one small window overlooking the camp. Austria is beautiful, with green hills and an open sky. But inside, the room was dark. It contained bunk beds, a kitchen table and chairs, a hot plate, and little else. The entire family slept, ate, and lived in the small room. I drank my third cup of Turkish coffee in an hour. It was an extravagance the families could little afford to share, but each pressed it on me, and I gratefully accepted their generous hospitality, though I never drank coffee, or anything with caffeine for that matter.

We finally entered the last room. I took off my shoes outside the door, pulled on a handmade pair of slippers, and sat down at the table. I met a woman in her 30s who shyly offered me a cup

of chai tea. I sipped it, but soon forgot that I even held a drink in my hand as she shared her story. The interpreter translated the horrific details.

"I gathered my children in the middle of the night. We climbed into a large truck that normally carried cargo. We were packed so tightly that it was nearly impossible to breathe. I had nothing but the clothes that I wore and money to pay the driver. My husband remained behind to avoid suspicion. He planned to join us later. As we traveled many of us became sick because there wasn't enough air and the road was rough."

She paused, composed herself, and resumed her story. She and her children scrambled off the truck when it stopped to allow them a bathroom break. After only a few moments, the driver called them back. She grabbed the hand of one of her children and climbed back into the sweltering confines of the cargo truck. She looked around frantically to find her other children, who were supposed to be behind her.

The doors shut just as she realized that her youngest son was not in the truck. As the motor started, she shouted for help. People beat on the sides of the truck.

"No one heard us," she said. "There was nothing that I could do."

Five years had passed. She showed me a picture of her young son and of her husband. Though she had worked with team members from mission groups and international relief organizations to find her missing family, her husband and son were never located. She refused to believe they might be dead, hoping that her husband somehow found her young son and that they are together. That is hope that makes sense, for sometimes there were miracles in the camp. It didn't happen often, but just recently a new refugee had arrived. He was greeted by the shouts of his grandfather. The whole camp celebrated the reunion of a family member once thought dead and the joy of an old man who thought he had no one left to call his own.

As I left the camp, my thoughts swirled. I thought about the people who crept away in the middle of the night in hope of finding safety. Many live for years in temporary refugee camps such as the one I visited in Austria while they wait for government papers to clear. Others leave to find new shelter when their allotted time has passed. Some are forced to go back to countries to begin again. Others, like my new friend, were afraid to leave. She fears that if she leaves the paper trail will diminish and her husband or son won't be able to locate her. That night, as I traveled to my hostel on the train, my hands shook. Several Turkish coffees and chai teas made my heart race and my hands tremble. But that was nothing compared to how I was shaking on the inside.

I had spent a day with people who had given all—literally.

The challenge of giving

> *Jesus shows his followers the pathway to a happy and satisfied heart. He tells us what makes life meaningful and rich. It is just so contrary to what the world says, so paradoxical to our own way of thinking, that even most of us who call ourselves Christians don't actually believe it.*[1]
>
> LESLIE VERNICK, FIFTYSOMETHING CHRISTIAN COUNSELOR AND AUTHOR

We live in an uneven world. Six million children under the age of 5 die every year from hunger. One hundred-thirty-four million children between the ages of 7 and 18 have never been to school. HIV/AIDS has created more than 14 million orphans—92 percent of them live in Africa.[2] Poverty, war, and disease claim many on this earth. And yet there are people living on the same planet who are unhealthy due to overconsumption—who spend millions trying to lose weight. People buy purses considered must-have, with price tags of $2000. You can win a game show on TV

in one 19-minute segment and carry home a quarter of a million dollars. In the faith world, there are sermons preached on prosperity; in fact, whole doctrines are wrapped around the idea of giving so you can receive fivefold, tenfold, and a hundredfold back when you give.

In my own life I sometimes forget what I have, holding on to what I could so freely give. In those moments I fail to appreciate how rich I am—not in dollars that accumulate in a bank account, but in wealth that will never register on Wall Street.

The ultimate giver is defined by James: "Real religion, the kind that passes muster before God the Father, is this: Reach out to the homeless and loveless in their plight, and guard against corruption from the godless world."[3]

There are good people and organizations working diligently around the world to make a difference in the lives of others. Many of them do not profess to know God. I am humbled when I realize that they have seized the joy of giving, but I am still struggling, though I have been granted so much by the greatest giver of all.

For me, I had to redefine the word *giving*. Giving isn't annual fund-raisers, or church contributions or even charity donated to worthy causes. These are a few ways that we give, but true giving is a way of living. Mark Allan Powell, in *Giving to God*, believes that being faithful as a giver means that you put your faith into action; he calls this stewardship, or "putting God in charge of everything." He writes,

> We believe that all we are and all that we have belongs to God and we believe that this is good news. Stewardship is about discovering the practical value of faith. The creeds and confessions that we cite are not just words and talk; they are prescriptions for experiencing life at its best. Being a faithful steward does not necessarily mean being a person who is a major donor to churches or charities, or being a person who is reluctant to spend

> money on his or her own pleasures or concerns. Rather, a faithful steward is a person who a) views the world as God's good creation and is grateful to be a part of it; b) knows that God cares for those whom God has made and is ready and willing to rule their lives; and c) trusts God to provide him or her with whatever is needed to make him or her content.[4]

Hey, do I have to give *everything*?

Mark tells how a young man ran to Jesus and knelt in front of him. He asked Jesus, "What shall I do to inherit eternal life?" This was an important question, for the rich young ruler lived by Jewish Law. He maintained a moral life. In essence, he was asking, "Look at my life and see if I'm doing everything I should."

Jesus said, "You know the commandments. Don't kill. Don't commit adultery. Don't steal or lie or commit fraud. Honor your father and mother."

The young man said, "I have done all of these things since I was a boy."

Jesus looked upon the young man with love and said, "There is one thing that you lack. Go and take everything that you own; sell it and give it to the poor. Then you'll have treasure in heaven. You can come and follow me."[5]

In typical fashion, Christ went beneath the surface to see the heart of the young man standing before him. Rather than look at the to-do list of the young man, he lovingly found the one area that was not on display for man to see.

The Scriptures say that the rich young ruler walked away in sorrow. It appears that Christ had asked too much. This story is often portrayed as a lesson on possessions, focusing on what the young man was unable to give. Instead, Jesus pointed out the young man's need, saying: "This is the one thing *you* lack."

The rich young ruler had enthusiasm. He respected Christ.

He knew how to follow the rules. The one thing he could not give was to place wealth and possessions in their proper place. He could not accept the invitation to discover what it meant to put it all down to follow Christ.

I don't know if Christ would have required the young man to give away all of his possessions, but I know that I consistently lay down things in my life that seem to have great value, only to discover that they meant less to me than what I gained by stripping them of their significance. Instead of asking what more can *I* do, I find freedom when I ask, "What more can you do in me?" If the young man was looking for ways to give strictly through the law, then Jesus gave him the opportunity to do so, but if he wanted to become an ultimate giver, then Christ gave him that opportunity as well.

Can I be honest?

It would be easier for me to pretend that I never struggle with this. It would make me shine brighter in your esteem if I didn't continue to struggle even after seeing people in tremendous need. But part of my giving is that I will never hide behind pretenses in order to gain the favor of people. I can't conquer this unless I'm honest, so I place it before God (and now you) openly so that he can continue his work in me.

I'm a giver in many ways. I am happy to donate my time to a good cause. I love to open my home to others. I love giving gifts; and little things make me happy, as I don't desire or want to accumulate "stuff." I am compelled to give sums of money to the man holding a sign on the street corner that says, "I'm hungry." I don't worry about whether it will go to a warm bed or if he will spend it on alcohol. I see the state of his clothing. I see that his teeth have not been cared for. The meager dollars are not a fair trade for his dignity, or the fact that he stands on a street corner in the cold.

But sometimes I battle offering benevolence toward people that I believe to be unkind or unfair. I often place high standards of behavior upon others that are impossible to meet, instead of giving grace. I have struggled to forgive injustice from my past, desiring to hold on to my feelings, rather than extend mercy. Each of these are areas in which Christ has stepped in and said, "The one thing that you lack, Suzie, is to give me this. Will you give it all?"

> "The mental process of giving myself to God seems easy to me. It's the actual working out of it that's hard, as well as being hard to see at times. I can easily say that I've given my dreams to God, but the moments I'm supposed to choose God's way above my dreams pass without notice. After all, God gave me the dream in the first place, I think. Shouldn't I pursue it?"
>
> Katie Hart, twentysomething

And I do. I give it to him as often as I need until my heart changes. I have found that the reward I receive is far greater than the meager recompense I pocket by holding on, but sometimes I'm still a work in progress.

Tithing is one way to express my faith; I approach it as an act of worship. I believe it to be biblical, and therefore I don't give out of guilt. But sometimes I think about what I could spend the money on. *Wouldn't this be a great way to save? What about buying a nicer car? Wouldn't it be nice to build a little extra in my checking account?* I understand the blessings that I have—health, loved ones, deep happiness—but I don't pretend that these are tied to my tithing like a kite on a string. What I do know is that this is my Achilles heel in the act of giving. I have asked God for help, and he is performing a work in me. Funny, but this miracle is actually taking place in the time when I have the least security financially. God is somehow showing me how to give not just my money, but my heart as I give.

Mark Allan Powell, in an interview about his book *Giving to God,* says this is a struggle many people have. He sought ways to make the Sunday offering a more meaningful part of his worship

experience. Instead of giving on Sunday morning, he mails in his offering as if it were an electric bill. Then he gets creative.

> Every week, I try to find one thing that I can do without—and give the money to God instead. It might be something little (like a dessert), or it could be something big, but I think about it every day until I decide what I am going to do. As a result, the offering has become my favorite part of the Sunday service. I would go to church just for that, to give God the little gift that I decided on earlier in the week.[6]

Why give?

Too often giving is characterized as a money-only issue. It's not about what we give, but the attitude in which we give—or the choice not to give when we should or could. Becoming a giver not only makes us aware of needs outside our own, but has the potential to transform our attitude as we give. Gary Thomas, founder of the Center for Evangelical Spirituality, describes an assignment he received to write an article on the topic of selflessness:

> After turning in the first draft, I received an e-mail back from the editor. He praised the work, but asked that I expand a section addressing the "rewards" of selflessness. The irony made me laugh. "Okay, I'll be unselfish," the thinking goes, "but if I do it, what's in it for me?"[7]

What will I get out of this? It's a question I've heard many times. From attending a church to giving time to a charitable organization to offering forgiveness, the core issue is not what will be given, but what is received in return.

I participated in an uncomfortable conversation the other day. One person described an event where money was collected for the children whose parents couldn't afford clothing and school supplies. "Why aren't the parents working?" he said. "I work 40 hours a week! If I give them money, then I keep them in the same cycle. What's in that for me?" He went on to describe all the reasons that he wouldn't give, including drug addiction of parents, government assistance, and more. I glanced around at our comfortable environment. My stomach was full. The room was comfortably cooled. My clothing wasn't threadbare, and if I wanted to go out and spend a small sum of money, I could. This person wasn't a bad person. Perhaps his point is that we should be responsible with giving, but sometimes the act of giving is less about the receiver than it is allowing God to ignite compassion within us toward those in need.

> "This reminds me of a song that begins with, 'I'm giving you my dreams, I'm laying down my rights for the promise of new life.' As for me, I'm okay with giving up money, almost too much so according to some people. It's more giving up time. I think I could be doing something else. For some reason, time just seems more important to me than money."
>
> ANNIE ZLOMKE, TWENTYSOMETHING

Time after time you hear the heartbeat of God as he commands us to take care of the widows, feed the hungry, and take care of those who are in need. The attitude of *What's in it for me?* is at odds with that directive, for most times there is nothing in it personally for you. It's sacrificial, which is what makes it a gift.

Serve me

This same outlook can also cross over into church. In the past five years I've watched discontent rise among many twentysomethings. For the most part this excites me! Discontent can be a powerful catalyst for change. These men and women want more than just sitting on a pew. They want to be active in their community. They want to talk about their faith over a latte. They want to be honest and open about their faith journey. They want church

to mean something, much like the New Testament church. I've had many interesting dialogues with friends, and I pray that God will empower this emerging church. I believe they will change the perception of Christianity in our nation!

But I've also prayed over a growing number of people who view discontent as an opportunity to criticize, instead of effect change. *Why don't they understand the traditional church isn't working for my generation? Don't they realize we want something different? Why would the pastor say that? Doesn't he realize how ridiculous he sounds to the rest of the world?* These are great questions and need to be asked, but what might happen if they were paired with these questions: *What can I do to bring change? What can I give to help this pastor reach my generation? How can I pray? God, what is my part?* The entire church might be changed if every person, no matter what age, walked into church and asked, *What do I have to offer? How can I worship you today? How can I thank you for the blessings I've received the other six days a week?*

Giving is first an attitude. An attitude of giving has the power to change others, change circumstances, and revolutionize our hearts, all motivated by sincere love for God.

Giving vs. Gucci

The reality is that getting is much more fun, at least that's what we are told. Jimmy Choo, Vera Wang, Gucci, Prada. It's not easy being a giver in a world full of gorgeous shoes, fabulous bags, and the perfect "look." But what happens when your identity as biblical women is at odds with the role of money and possessions in your life? Which do you choose?

Giving or Gucci?

I love leather high heels with pointed toes. Tall black boots. Shoes that are comfortable (or not so comfortable) yet stylish. Do you see a trend developing? But these do not identify me or consume me. They are not my identity marker, and I would put them down tomorrow if they threatened to take on more importance in my life than they should. But that doesn't mean I don't struggle with giving in other ways.

Is it wrong to have nice things?

Jesus said, "I came so they can have real and eternal life, more and better life than they ever dreamed of."[8] Another version calls it "abundant" life. This is a gift from God that has nothing to do with entertainment or possessions. It's an identity mark that is greater than any fashion statement on the cover of *Vogue* or any design showcased on the latest Paris runway. Like Paul, you have the opportunity to find genuine contentment. In Philippians 4 he says, "Actually, I don't have a sense of needing anything personally. I've learned by now to be quite content whatever my circumstances."

Contentment is happiness that can't be taken away by your situation. It's experiencing peace that doesn't make sense when life turns upside down. It's learning to give generously out of your abundance—whether that is abundance of spirit or family or faith or finances.

Creative ways to give

Giving doesn't come naturally for the majority of people. It becomes second nature only after you begin to give. So, where do you begin?

1. You give thanks.
2. You give time.
3. You give of your talent.
4. You give sacrificially.
5. You give to those in need.

Let's start giving!

Take a moment and acknowledge those who have affirmed

you, believed in you when you didn't believe in yourself, or who pushed you when you wanted to give up. Make a phone call. Send a note (handwritten, not e-mail or text). Give a hug that is unexpected, or take them out for dinner. Your list might be long, which will allow you to give thanks on a regular basis.

Give of your time. Donate an hour to clean the home of an elderly person. Offer to be a Big Sister to a young girl (www.bbbs.org). Clean out your closet and donate your nicely used clothes to a shelter. Offer to volunteer in your community or perhaps even overseas. You can find a nationwide databank of opportunities at Volunteer Match (www.volunteermatch.org/).

Give of your talents. Make a meal for someone who is sick. Make a scrapbook for a friend. Make a video to encourage someone who needs a laugh, or a hug. Write a song or paint a picture for someone as a gift. Teach a child to play soccer. Volunteer to teach someone how to read through a literacy program.

Give sacrificially. Go out of your way to be kind to someone who is disagreeable. Give random hugs. Offer to carry something heavy for someone. Smile. Forgive that friend or family member, even if they don't know how to receive it. Do something without expecting anything back. Hold back criticism or gossip when everything in you wants to give it away.

Give to those in need. Instead of a birthday gift, ask friends and family to donate toward a water well for a community in an impoverished region. Buy groceries for a food bank. One loaf of bread, a jar of peanut butter, and a jar of jelly will make a difference. Give your old cell phone or computer away to charities that turn these items into cash for their programs. Give blood. Get a haircut and donate your hair to Locks of Love, an organization that creates wigs for children with cancer, or adopt a child through Compassion International.*

The key to becoming a giver is to give. To do something without expecting anything back, including a thank-you. That's

* Find out more at www.locksoflove.org; www.compassion.org.

when you and I discover what Leslie Vernick, in *How to Find Selfless Joy in a Me-First World,* calls a virtue:

> Like Pinocchio, I have to come to understand that the virtue of humility, or selflessness, provides a more fertile ground for personal, relational, and spiritual joy than does working toward self-improvement, self-esteem, or self-fulfillment.[9]

Or in other words, abundant living.

Write a personal definition of giving.

____

____

Do you ever struggle with giving? In what area?

____

____

The rich young ruler invited Christ to examine the area in which he lacked. Are you willing to do the same? Write your thoughts to God.

____

____

What does it mean to you to be "content in all things"?

____

____

There's no way that one person can give enough to change a world, but what might happen if we all became givers? What is one way you desire to give?

____

____

I want to have a giving spirit, God. I desire to put it all down so that I can find what I need through you. You know my weaknesses, and you know where I love to give. Let me give you those frail areas of my being. Let me delight you as I give willingly. Help me to be content where I am and with what I have, and to bless others in many different ways. Thank you for shaping my heart as I give with my hands and all that I am.

Actually, I don't have a sense of needing anything personally. I've learned by now to be quite content whatever my circumstances. I'm just as happy with little as with much, with much as with little. I've found the recipe for being happy whether full or hungry, hands full or hands empty. Whatever I have, wherever I am, I can make it through anything in the One who makes me who I am.

FROM PHILIPPIANS 4

PART FOUR: FUTURE

Vocation is the road less traveled

The disciples went everywhere preaching,
the Master working right with them, validating
the Message with indisputable evidence.
FROM MARK 16

Blog

What about me?

Current mood: anxious to go

As a teenager, if anyone had told me that as a college student I would be standing in Kharkov, Ukraine (part of the former Soviet Union), I probably would have laughed. I was there to help people new in their faith learn more about the Bible. But I discovered just what a short, timid girl was truly capable of when she turned everything over to God. That summer was the beginning of my destiny.

But if someone had asked me back then where I would be in 10 or 15 years, I would have answered, "In Ukraine or in Russia or perhaps even in Africa. I will be married, raising my children, using my education degree to gain access into closed countries." So where am I now? I live in the United States with my husband and our one- and three-year-olds. I teach Pre-K at a child-care center.

Maybe I'm in what my pastor calls a "holding pattern" because at this point, I can't see my destiny anywhere but in my dreams. It seems so far away that I wonder if I'll ever get there. I teeter back and forth between faith that God knows what He is doing and thoughts of doubt and confusion. Did I hear God correctly?

Sometimes I feel forgotten. But then moments come when God gives me a glimpse of the future and I resolve, once again, not to give up on my dreams or myself. And then I have to see what has been placed right in front of me today. I can listen to someone and share what God has taught me. Or truly see the children God has placed in my care—my own, and those in my preschool class. They will only be with me for a while, and I have a tremendous impact on their futures.

God is putting all the pieces of the puzzle together. He loves me enough not to forget about me, just as I don't forget about my children or quit dreaming big dreams for them.

There is a future, and my path to that future is carved out by what I do today.

Sarah Ballard, thirtysomething

TEN

Vocation—what is it? Why is it crucial?

EVERY TIME MY HUSBAND, Richard, meets someone, a conversation like this begins:

"Have I met you before?" he asks.

"Not sure," the person replies.

"Where are you from?"

That begins a game of connect-the-dots. The other person names their home city. Richard throws out a name of someone he knows from that city or town, and eventually the *aha* moment occurs. "I knew his father's brother..." or, "I played basketball with her cousin."

Richard is a genius at finding the common connection. It once happened on a plane trip to Bangladesh. Another time on the way to Brazil.

It also happens in random places. I sat beside him while he recuperated after having his wisdom teeth taken out. He was in la-la land after the anesthesia, but managed to hold a riveting conversation with one of the nurses. Within moments, he found more than one connection.

Later, he didn't even remember the conversation.

It's a gene he received from his grandmother. I was shopping once with her at a small grocery store in her community. A woman walked by, and Grandmother pointed her cane at her. "That's a MacIntosh, if I ever saw one," she said.

I watched as she hunted down the woman, and then waited as they talked for a half hour. The woman did not consider Grandmother a stalker, for it turns out she *was* a MacIntosh—three times removed! Grandmother knew more about the woman's family than she did. As we exited the store, Grandmother smiled. "I knew she was a MacIntosh," she said. "You can just tell by looking."

My daughter Melissa was in Durban, South Africa, to work with a missionary family for eight weeks. She was a long way from home. Melissa didn't know anyone in South Africa, and her first week was spent getting acquainted with the family. One night they sat around the table when Joel (the missionary) received a phone call from the States. It was from his old mentor, an aged pastor in Texas. The pastor was excited and couldn't wait to share the news with Joel.

The pastor's grandson and his wife had graduated from college and were barely scraping along, working full-time for a part-time paycheck at a tiny church. The pastor had been praying for his grandson, and just that day a church called to offer his grandson a job. The pay was great, but more than that, the job appeared to be custom-made for the couple. When Joel hung up he shared the details with his family, not mentioning the location and name of the pastor.

Melissa listened, frowning. It sounded familiar. "Where did you say this was?"

Joel shared the city and church, and Melissa laughed out loud.

It was *her* church and *her* pastor, thousands of miles away from Durban, South Africa.

What were the odds?

What is a vocation?

> *Desires of their heart. We all have them, but for some reason or another, have not been taught what to do with them. We don't know how to implement what we know of God and who we know him to be into our daily heart's desires. Most of all, I think we're afraid. Afraid if we offer them to him, maybe he won't give them to us. That's the most common denominator I have experienced with the myriads of women I've met.*
>
> KARYN LONG, THIRTYSOMETHING CO-FOUNDER OF THE AFTER EVE CONFERENCE

Me and you, and her, and her...

There are many words tossed about when people are trying to define the future: career, your lot in life, prospects, hope. One word I believe is a great fit is *vocation.* Parker J. Palmer, in *Let Your Life Speak,* defines a woman with a vocation as someone "who lives out her full self in the world."[1] Vocation is more than a job. It's more than a profession. It's more than how much money you'll make one day. It's finding your place in the world.

Here's where the idea of connection comes in. When you begin to live out your full self, you are bound to impact others, because the world is often a much smaller place than we imagine. In 1929, a Hungarian author named Frigyes Karinthy published a volume of short stories. One story was titled "Chain-Links." In it, Karinthy shared a belief that the modern world was shrinking due to the connectedness of human beings. This was possible due to technological advances in communications and travel, and growing friendship networks reaching over greater distances. In the story, Karinthy's characters believed that any two individuals could be connected through at most five acquaintances. The characters created a game out of this notion and bet that, using no more than five individuals, one of whom was a personal acquaintance, they could contact a selected person. This concept became known as "Six Degrees of Separation."

While the concept remains unproven, spiritually the theory is powerful. The ripples from your life affect others. God sees your future and even you in a way that you might not. He's not so much counting your virtues or winning personality as he is looking at you personally and the part you play in his plan. What plan is that? From Genesis to Revelation, God's overarching plan is to draw people to himself. Let's go back to the foundation of our faith: "God so loved the world that he gave his one and only son."

Ordinary people throughout time have been instrumental in that simple plan. The word *future* seems so big. Six little letters that carry so much weight. You prepare for your future, but sometimes it remains murky, teasing you, lingering just beyond your ability to grasp it. Will you consider these things?

1. Your vocation might take hard work.
2. Vocation is not a destination, but a lifelong process.
3. Your vocation might seem ordinary to others.

Birthing process

I met Karyn Long, a fun, chic, thirtysomething woman living in the D.C. area, when I spoke at a conference called After Eve in 2005. I arrived from the airport and drove to McLean Church, a megachurch that reaches thousands. Though I spoke at several different events throughout the year, I was especially excited to be a part of After Eve. The topics were relevant. These women weren't afraid to tackle the tough issues of the day in light of faith. The women were energized, hopeful, and excited about their future.

At that first conference, most of the speakers were younger than I, and throughout the weekend I listened in awe to these up-and-coming teachers, speakers, musical artists, as well as a popular female Christian comedian, Kerri Pomarolli. I wanted to applaud the small group of women who founded this conference as I watched their dream unfold.

The idea for the conference began two years earlier. It was a vision written down on a napkin in a restaurant. A woman named Amy Ehmann had approached Karyn and others about launching a seminar just for young women. Amy had talked with others, but Karyn was the first to catch the vision with her. Shortly after, others joined and the idea sprang to life. Karyn was enthused. This conference would address issues that were familiar.

"As a young woman in the Lord, at one time I was making decisions based on emotions and not on the Word, and it led to very poor outcomes. As I grew in my walk and his Word," says Karyn, "I realized God wanted to walk beside me and help me make biblically based decisions. My heart was for young women, standing firmly rooted and knowing it, and better yet, knowing him as a personally intimate God who desires to walk us through this life. After Eve was an avenue to 'mass-produce' this ability for young women across the country."

The task seemed overwhelming. There were a thousand menial details. There were times that Amy, Karyn, and the team felt snowed under. "I always felt unequipped," says Karyn. "I look back in my prayer journal. We began this journey two-and-a-half years before the Lord called it into being. We were walking by faith each step of the way. When I look in my journal I see a prayer almost weekly. 'Lord, please pick the speakers,' or 'Lord, we have no funds,' or 'Lord, please give us a name.' Every step was prayed for. And now I look back and see how he intimately and securely answered each one of them. Never did I feel completely equipped for my position in this conference. It was all God."

They initially hoped to reach around a hundred women in the first conference, and were surprised when over a thousand from around the country registered. Karyn remembers that time with amazement. "God humbled me by how truly big he really was, and is. I pray that the fear of the unknown never stops one of us from finding what God wants to do. I have found that it's the most adventuresome place to be."

Today, the After Eve conference continues to grow,* and the team of women are considering branching out, taking this same conference to other areas of North America.

It's not a place—it's a journey

Perhaps it seem like finding your place in the world is just outside your grasp. You feel God tugging at your heart. You're faithful. You're open to whatever God has for you right now, but also hopeful that your future will be made clear—soon!

While you live your calling as a woman of faith every day, your future or vocation is a long-range plan. It's finding your unique niche. It's a lifetime process, taking you through many years and many places. What is my unique niche? It's to be a communicator, but I didn't know that in my twenties. In fact, communication was a weakness. I would remain quiet rather than create conflict. I often avoided deeper conversations, not because I didn't love to participate, but because I was still learning who I was. I continued to live my calling daily. I stayed close to my heavenly father. The longer I knew him, the more I learned about myself. His simple plan slipped into my heart, and into my everyday life.

You may be the exact opposite. You know exactly what you want to do. You may be a lawyer, or your heart's desire is to be a mom. You may be well on your way up the career ladder, or firmly learning all that you need to work in the field of your choice. You're excited about what God is doing right now, but still have questions about how and when or where.

I've met women who are focused, who hold the reins tightly as they work their way toward their goals, sometimes eliminating the God factor as they fight their way to success. I've also met and befriended beautiful young women who seem bent on destroying their future, accepting far less than they should, giving up on a

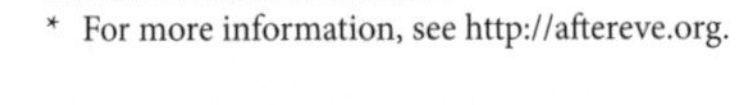

* For more information, see http://aftereve.org.

future because it seems too distant or too big. I've also met women patiently working through the discovery process.

Side by side, these women look a lot alike. The binding thread that runs through all of the stories is that God has a plan. The difference is letting God in on the journey. Finding your vocation is not "fate" or "karma." Everything we have, everything that we are, and therefore everything that we become can be directed by Christ, if we allow it. The good news is that nothing is wasted.

In my early twenties I was a mom and a wife. In my mid-twenties I worked as a secretary at an engineering firm. I loved my co-workers. I was learning. I was still growing, in both confidence and skills. I was promoted to a Tulsa office as part of a team to launch a new office. I assumed new responsibilities and a new title. I commuted. I worked longer hours. I gained more experience, more confidence. And something was happening inside of me. The raises were nice. The pats on the back were great, but just as powerful as open doors can be, there were doors closing in my heart.

Sometimes finding your vocation means that there are closed doors, as well as the open doors. I prayed for the right timing, and shortly after that I came home to write full-time. I had a lot of experience to gain. Many fledgling writers give up because this is a business based on rejection. Thousands of books are released every year, and few survive. But as I got closer to discovering my vocation I found that nothing is wasted. I wrote many proposals and presentations for city authority members when I worked for the firm. I wished that I were writing the next great novel or non-fiction book instead. I felt I was wasting time. What I didn't realize is that I was gaining skills that would be valuable later on in my vocation: Writing under deadline. Working with people. Managing multiple tasks. Exercising discipline to get the job done well.

All of these proved valuable.

You might believe that you're in a holding pattern, when

you are actually stocking up needed skills or character traits. If you don't believe that to be true, then begin to pray about where you hope to be, as you assess your life honestly. I talked with a friend and her husband the other day. He said, "I'm so unhappy with my job."

She said, "Then what is your goal? You say you are unhappy, but you don't make any moves."

He's doing. He's showing up every day. His wife asked a hard, but necessary question: Are you willing to stop doing, and start taking steps toward what you want to do? That might mean that you begin to explore your passions or your talents. It might mean reassessing the definition of success. If money is the definition of success, then I'm in the wrong business. It doesn't line up with my real self. But if my desire is to work so that I can give to others, then making money *is* the definition of success.

In *Let Your Life Speak: Listening for the Voice of Vocation,* Parker J. Palmer says, "Today I understand vocation quite differently—not as a goal to be achieved, but as a gift to be received. Discovering vocation does not mean scrambling towards some prize just beyond my reach but accepting the treasure of true self that I already possess."

I'm tired of waiting!

My friend Sarah is 33. She's a wife and a mom of two. She plans one day to be a missionary. She went to the university and gained her degree and teaching certificate, hoping that her degree would allow her entrance to countries that might not be open to her otherwise. Sometimes Sarah gets frustrated. She loves her two beautiful children, Caleb and Abi. She loves her husband, Darrin, but she wonders if her future has somehow slipped out of her reach.

But with history as our teacher, we see men and women finding their vocation over many years and through successes and failures. Great men and women in history—artists, authors, musicians,

leaders, scientists, and others—marched toward their vocation. Their paths were marked with disappointment, hard work, and victory. But they continued in their passion, and thus discovered what they were meant to do.

In Hebrews 11 we find a hall of fame of sorts. One verse says, "They saw it way off in the distance, waved their greeting, and accepted the fact that they were transients in this world."

These people's efforts weren't in vain. Though they didn't see immediate results, like petals lifted to the sky, their work bloomed in the lives and hearts of others long after their hands had ceased their labor. Your vocation is a lifelong process, revealed as you and I allow God to direct us, as we pursue our passions, and as we focus on what God desires in and through his creation.

The reality is that we live in seasons. Many of my friends developed their career or vocation first, and family second. Richard and I had our children young, and our vocations are being fulfilled later in life. But if vocation is a lifelong process, we are each running a long-distance race, and the finish line is the same.

> "Hebrews 11 has been big for me this year. Last year was the beginning of the Shermona faith journey. Not because I decided, 'Hey, it's time to increase your faith.' God said it was time. I have been in one situation after the other where all I could do is surrender and say, 'I trust you and I believe. Help me to do what you want me to do, and if there is any doubt, I want to believe.' When God says it is time, there is no stopping Him."
>
> SHERMONA, TWENTYSOMETHING

Your vocation might seem ordinary

A team is made up of players with different talents or abilities. Maybe one member is a wise counselor. Or another has great faith to believe for healing when someone is sick. Some are teachers. Others have the ability to lead others to Christ. Some are generous. Others have the ability to distinguish what builds

> "The people that came before us, I believe, lead the way for us today. Last Sunday in church, our pastor showed a video of a sweet old lady that had recently passed away. He wanted to show her passion for Christ. I sat in that service thinking. *I want to be like her. I want people to remember me like that.* And I got to thinking about the words in a song: '*I want to leave a legacy—how will they remember me?*' I think that the generation before us has paved the way and they are letting us take over and continue what they have started."
>
> MICHELLE PLUNKETT, TWENTYSOMETHING

up or tears down. You may have a heart of mercy and choose the counseling profession. Perhaps you are able to discern what is right or wrong, and choose to be a judge. But maybe you desire to work behind the scenes. You want to serve.

When our diverse gifts come together, the ripple effect swells to a tidal wave as genuine faith plays out in every area of our lives, spilling out, no matter where or what that is. Sometimes the words *vocation* or *destiny* are frustrating because we think it needs to be something extraordinary. Something grand. Paul doesn't mince words when he admonishes friends who lived in the city of Corinth:

> Take a good look, friends, at who you were when you got called into this life. I don't see many of "the brightest and the best" among you, not many influential, not many from high-society families. Isn't it obvious that God deliberately chose men and women that the culture overlooks and exploits and abuses, chose these "nobodies" to expose the hollow pretensions of the "somebodies"?[2]

When I travel, people often ask about my family. One time someone asked where my husband worked, and when I said that he worked at a factory, her eyebrows rose.

"Why? Are you surprised?" I asked.

"He isn't in ministry?" she asked.

Yes, he was. He still is. Richard worked for 18 years in a factory where a large number of people didn't know about Christ, or had misconceptions about Christianity. They got to see Richard under adverse situations daily—a bad boss or mandatory overtime or working in 100-plus degree heat around three-story machines that spewed dust and debris. He didn't plan to work there forever, but it was great training while he was there. He saw his co-workers as friends, and his time with them as important. It wasn't the crowds of 5000 attended by faithful believers longing to hear a famous preacher or speaker. His name wasn't on the cover of a book. He wasn't in the stage lights, and for the most part his faith-filled daily life wasn't applauded.

But the men and women he worked with respected him. They knew that when their family was in crisis that they could ask Richard to pray for them, and that he would. They knew that he stayed in a difficult job so that he could take care of his family, let our children run after their dreams, and encourage me in my "ministry."

This past year he left and is attending a university full-time. His plans are to finish the education he began years ago when we first met, and he has long-range goals and plans to achieve his master's and doctorate in counseling. Those men and women in his old job miss him. When he left, many shared with me that they saw Christ in the way that he lived. It was an ordinary situation. And yet God allowed him to live extraordinarily in that phase of his life. Those relationships enriched my husband; they are his friends. And that's how Christ lived. With purpose. To serve. To obey his heavenly father.

Believe big, but allow God to define what big looks like.

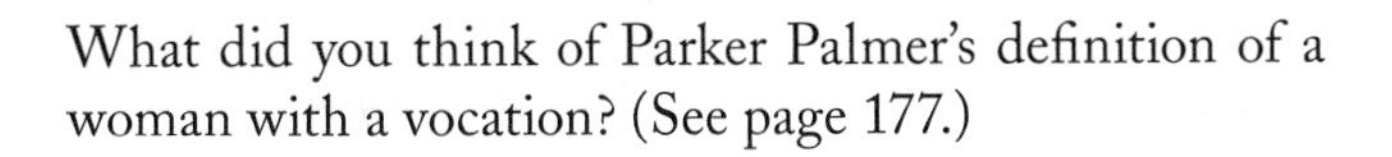

What did you think of Parker Palmer's definition of a woman with a vocation? (See page 177.)

____

____

What is one frustration you've encountered when considering your future?

____

____

Do you believe that a vocation is a lifelong process? Why or why not?

____

____

Have you ever had doors closed? Did you consider that it might be an answer, rather than a rejection?

____

____

Think about your past experiences. How can these experiences be useful in your vocation? (This can be work experience or life experience.)

____

____

Jesus, I live fully when I find my real self, the one you know better than I. Peel away everything that distracts me from finding my vocation. Shut doors, and let me gracefully let them close. Open doors and give me courage to walk through them. Thank you that you have gifted me. If it is serving, let me serve. If it is teaching, let me teach. If it is leading, let me lead. I look forward to living my full self in the world over many years, and in many places.

Passing along the beach of Lake Galilee, he saw Simon and his brother Andrew net-fishing. Fishing was their regular work. Jesus said to them, "Come with me. I'll make a new kind of fisherman out of you. I'll show you how to catch men and women instead of perch and bass." They didn't ask questions. They dropped their nets and followed.

FROM MARK 1

Blog

Something in store for me

Current mood: excited

I have always felt that people have held me to a different standard. If I messed up or did something wrong, it was okay because I had been through so much. Yet if I did something right it was always kind of shocking, maybe even a fluke.

You see, when I was not quite a teenager, my parents were sent to prison. I bounced from friend's house to friend's house staying wherever I could, even in cars. Living like this, I got involved with some scary stuff, following in my parents' footsteps. Gangs, drugs, older guys, being arrested. One of the places I stayed, however, led me to a Christian camp, where I met Christ as my Savior, and life has never been the same since.

For a long time I feel like I was letting other people decide my destiny for me, when they treated me like that. But then I realized that my true destiny has already been decided for me! God has written it, and he expects and hopes for the best out of me. He is not shocked that I turned out normal.

I am only 24 years old, and God has done so much through me already. I have had the opportunity to speak to hundreds of people all over the country, bringing many to know him. I have been to Mexico, Africa, and Europe on mission trips. I have worked with troubled youth. I also have the most amazing family of my own—a husband of six years and two precious little boys. I don't know what God has in store next, but I know it's going to be great. And if he can do all this through me, he can work through anyone.

Sometimes it is so hard to figure out what's next. What is my destiny? I think as long as you have an open heart and willing hands, it will come to you. John Wesley said, "If we get on fire for the Lord, the world will come and watch us burn." That just gets me so excited—to think that all we have to do is stay close to him, and not worry, because he has us all destined for greatness!

Nichole Johnson, twentysomething

ELEVEN

Changing the world

I RAN AS FAST AS I COULD DOWN THE STREET. Rain pelted my skinny frame as I pushed through my exhaustion. I was soaked. I was cold and barefoot. I was 13. I ran all the way to McClure Park, several blocks from my home. I stopped, my hands on my knees, my breath coming in short gasps. I wanted to run away, but I knew that I had no money, no place to go. So I turned around and walked back home.

If you had approached that soaking-wet, crying girl, and told her that one day she'd be an author, travel around the world speaking, have the family she hoped for, be completely content with life, passionate, and adventurous, I'm sure she would have stared at you in disbelief. You see, that little girl believed that her destiny was created by her circumstances, or perhaps by other people's choices. She couldn't see past her feelings, or the fact that life wasn't always fair. She looked around and it appeared that others were marked with destiny, while she was only marked.

I no longer resemble that hurting girl. I remember her, but I see the miracles that have happened in her life, not only in her, but in her family. She is the reason I started working with teens in my early twenties. She is the reason that I will never take my faith for granted. I've had the privilege of watching her embrace who she is and discover that destiny is knowing God.

A friend is a chaplain at a local jail. Each week she sits with women and shares that God loves them. Several years ago my friend was a prisoner in the same jail. Women from our church visited her and others. She was an addict. It was a battle that had raged for 20 years, and she felt hopeless, but after the women left she began to read her Bible. For days, she hungrily read the words she found inside.

Prison didn't have the power to change her. She faced a long jail sentence. Outside of jail, circumstances had only pushed her deeper into addiction. The women who visited her in jail didn't even know how to make things better. Their words were thought provoking, but still hope seemed very far away once they left.

But after several days of reading the Bible, hope tiptoed in, and she found herself on her face talking to a God she thought had abandoned her. That changed her. He changed her. In a dark prison cell, she saw God for the first time.

One year after her release from prison, I asked my new friend to write a letter. I asked her to share the one thing that she would have wanted to say before she knew Christ. This is what she wrote:

> Dear church people,
>
> I understand that some of you have been sent to tell us about God. I've heard a little about him. In case I get to meet you, there are just a few things I'd like to ask. I know about hell because I'm pretty sure I already live there. I know about judgment because people who don't understand my life judge me every day.
>
> But maybe we could talk about repentance, because I don't know how to do that. I've heard that your God's kindness will lead a person to forgiveness, so maybe if I could just meet him, he would show me that kindness, and then you wouldn't have to explain. You see, some

> of us are not only lost, but we're addicts too, and it's no longer a choice for us. Perhaps you can show me that mercy I've heard about, a mercy that sets people free.
>
> If your God is really like that, will you tell me?
>
> Signed, Kim[1]

> *God's Spirit is on me; he's chosen me to preach the Message of good news to the poor, sent me to announce pardon to prisoners and recovery of sight to the blind, to set the burdened and battered free.*
>
> Jesus reading the prophetic scrolls, as recorded by Luke

Getting to business

I read an article today that dissected my faith, examining it like a cadaver under bleak and harsh lights. The author talked about the politics of Christianity—far right vs. fundamentalism vs. Christian majority. It highlighted the weaknesses of men who fell from great heights of ministry, pointing out the flaws and excess of hypocrisy. It pointed to those who hold signs of hatred at funerals and shout out curses and epithets in the name of Christianity.

It portrayed my faith in a bleak light. There are elements of truth in some of these accusations. Christianity is comprised of ordinary men and women, and many are at different levels in their faith journey. Some have much to learn, while others grasp bits and pieces of Scripture and fail to portray the whole truth. Some are misinformed, or zealous without compassion. They forget what Christ said in John 13:

> Let me give you a new command: Love one another. In the same way I loved you, you love one another. This is

> how everyone will recognize that you are my disciples—
> when they see the love you have for each other.[2]

If you don't know God, you might only see the people—flawed and full of faults—or the institution with rituals and committee meetings. But the church is comprised of thousands and thousands of men and women of integrity, who don't profess perfection, but their faith is integral in their life. There are those whose life is marked by faith, like my friend the chaplain, who found wholeness and joy when she opened her life to Christ. There are Christians who volunteer in their community, on missions trips, and quietly put their faith in action in ways that will never be seen in a newspaper headline, such as the person who once put a hundred-dollar bill in my mailbox when we were struggling financially.

When you consider these variations, it's understandable why some are confused. I recently read this on a blog. It was an anonymous comment—one person's definition of a believer:

> Christians—those people on TV and in government who are always judging and condescending. Not to be confused with christians (lower case "c") who are feeding the hungry, visiting the sick, clothing the poor, consoling the heartbroken, standing up to the Man in support of the People. You find Christians on TV and in public office calling us to action; you find christians in the poorest areas of your city handing out food and clothing and along the US/Mexico border handing out water.

When I see how my faith appears from the outside looking in, it drives me to my knees in prayer and to the Scripture for understanding. I long to be able to share the right words, to explain the joy of what it means to be intimate with God. I want to share the heart of Christianity, which is that lives are changed when there is an encounter with Christ.

It's why I write. It's why I speak, or why I sit one-on-one with

someone, or wrap my arm around her. It's why I say I'm sorry when I'm wrong, and fall to my knees when I see my shortcomings. It's why I can't be afraid to talk about my faith, even when it's misunderstood, for we live in a thirsty world.

And I've met someone who has what they seek.

If you are thirsty

Every year the University of Texas and the University of Oklahoma meet for a showdown. The streets are crowded. Loyalty runs high. There are bumper stickers, Texas Longhorn signs, and a wash of crimson and cream on the Sooner side. For Oklahoma and Texas, it's just as big as the Super Bowl.

A couple of thousand years ago, there was a Jewish celebration that was just as impressive called the Feast of Tabernacles. Every Jewish family who lived within 20 miles of the city was required to leave their homes to build a booth or a tent in order to remember their ancestors and the journey they took out of slavery. This festival was like a national champion pre-game event. People paraded through the streets singing songs. They performed sacrifices every day of the week.

The eighth day was the Super Bowl of the feast! The priests led thousands to the pool of Siloam in a parade. People followed, dancing, singing songs of praise. At the pool of Siloam, the priest dipped a golden pitcher in the water and poured the water over an altar. It was a symbolic act to remind God of his promises.

As this scene plays out, we notice a carpenter's son standing quietly on the edge of the crowd observing. At the moment that the priest poured out the symbolic water, Jesus cried out in a very loud voice,

> If anyone thirsts, let him come to me and drink. Rivers of living water will brim and spill out of the depths of anyone who believes in me this way, just as the Scripture says.[3]

His message was intense. So much so, that he interrupted the rituals. He diverted their attention away from a golden pitcher filled with dank water to let them know that living water was available, if only they would come to him to drink. He was telling them the very thing they prayed for was right there, in their midst.

There were many different people in the crowd that day. Listen to their reactions. Some said, "Is this guy a prophet?" The seekers said, "Is he real?" Others believed he was the Christ. *Is it really true? The Christ is here!* Others mocked him, saying, "Isn't this the man who lives in Galilee?" The crowd argued, divided by their opinions of the man on the sidelines.[4]

Doesn't that sound familiar? You and I live in a thirsty world. People are looking for answers to the bigger questions, and yet many people feel as if it is impossible to find them. They might be confused by your faith. They might even be angry. Every person in the crowd that day had an opportunity to hear the message and respond personally. Why didn't they? The reality is that if you haven't tasted living water, you might not know just how great it is.

Perhaps you have some misconceptions of your own. Spiritually, you want to know God. You are seeking a definition of biblical womanhood, trying to sort through the cultural definitions to hear the voice of God. You desire to live your faith outside the church in tangible ways. But it seems hard. You ask, "Is it possible for me to change the world?"

The answer is no, it's not. But Jesus can—through you. Jesus made this promise: "Whoever believes in me, as the Scripture has said, streams of living water will flow from within him."[5]

Something happens when you come to Christ. The living water that Jesus offered (and still offers today) is from the depths of his love. It supplies the new believer, or even the very religious, with light, life, love, and freedom. This produces something new in you. It's a word that I have come to love, that I pray to be in my

own life. It's called *agapao,* the word that means that God lives inside of you in such measure that others are drawn to him.

Jesus told the crowd that day, "Drink this water and not only will your thirst be quenched, but you will overflow." The intimacy that you have with God can be so real that it will extend to others like a running fountain. Look around you. There are a lot of hurdles in our way when we're trying to live out our faith. We can complain about that. We can point out people's faults, ignoring our own, or we can show them Christ as we focus on the one standing at the edge of the crowd, speaking in a loud voice: *If you are thirsty, come to me.*

In closing

May I pray with you as we end this awesome conversation?

> *Father, I thank you for this beautiful twentysomething woman. Thank you for who she is, but more so, thank you for what you are doing in her life. Fill her today with your promises. Live inside of her in such a way that others are drawn to you. Thank you for my new friend.*

Let's keep talking!

I WANT TO HEAR FROM YOU. If you desire to keep this conversation going, here are a few ways we can keep in touch:

ShoutLife: http://shoutlife.com/suzanneeller

Facebook: www.facebook.com; ID: T. Suzanne Eller

MySpace: http://myspace.com/suzanneeller

Dare to Believe: http://daretobelieve.org—my Web site

Boomer Babes Rock!: www.boomerbabesrock.com. If you want to check in with me and some of my awesome friends you met in this book, you can connect with me, Allison Bottke, and others as we talk about life, love, faith, relationships, destiny, and more!

T. Suzanne Eller's other books

Real Teens, Real Stories, Real Life

Real Issues, Real Teens: What Every Parent Needs to Know

The Mom I Want to Be: Rising Above Your Past to Give Your Kids a Great Future

Making It Real: Whose Faith Is It Anyway?

MORE RESOURCES

Image

You Matter More Than You Think by Dr. Leslie Parrott

Wanting to Be Her: Body Image Secrets Victoria Won't Tell You by Michelle Graham

How People Grow by Dr. Henry Cloud and Dr. John Townsend

Relationships

Adventures in Holy Matrimony by Julie Ann Fidler

Red-Hot Monogamy by Bill and Pam Farrel

Friendlationships by Jeff Taylor

Single Wisdom by Paris M. Finner-Williams

Undressed: The Naked Truth About Love, Sex and Dating by Jason Illian

Boundaries by Dr. Henry Cloud and Dr. John Townsend

Spiritual growth

Every Thought Captive: Battling the Toxic Beliefs That Separate Us from the Life We Crave by Jerusha Clark

Having a Mary Heart in a Martha World by Joanna Weaver

Having a Mary Spirit by Joanna Weaver

From Faking It to Finding Grace by Connie Cavanaugh

Finding Selfless Joy in a Me-First World by Leslie Vernick

Listen by Keri Wyatt Kent

Breathe by Keri Wyatt Kent

Oxygen by Keri Wyatt Kent

Marked For Life by Crystal Miller

Giving to God: The Bible's Good News About Living a Generous Life by Mark Allan Powell

Just for you

Twentysomething: Surviving and Thriving in the Real World by Margaret Feinberg

Perspectives: A Spiritual Life Guide for Twentysomethings by Colin Creel

Finding God Beyond Harvard by Kelly Monroe Kullberg

Confessions of a Pastor by Craig Groeschel

20-Something, 20-Everything by Christine Hassler

You can make a difference

The Gutter by Craig Gross

Let Your Life Speak: Listening for the Voice of Vocation by Parker J. Palmer

Conferences for young women

After Eve—http://aftereve.org

She Speaks—www.shespeaksconference.com

Hearts at Home (for young moms)—http://heartsathomeorg

NOTES

Let's create a village

1. Shirin Taber, *Wanting All the Right Things* (Orlando, FL: Relevant Books, 2006), 17.
2. Taber, 18.

Chapter 1—Woman under construction?

1. See Exodus 3:2-10.
2. Jerusha Clark, *Every Thought Captive* (Colorado Springs, CO: TH1NK Books, NavPress, 2006), 37.
3. See Joshua 1:5.
4. Crystal Miller, *Marked for Life* (Colorado Springs, CO: TH1NK Books, NavPress, 2006), 97.
5. Keri Wyatt Kent, *Listen* (Somerset, NJ: Jossey-Bass, 2006), 45.
6. 1 Timothy 1:14.
7. See Exodus 4:1-22.
8. Acts 7:21-22 NLT, emphasis added.

Chapter 2—Where do I fit?

1. Chris Wadsworth, "Reality Bytes," The *News-Press, Jackson Sun,* 1/26/2006.
2. 2 Timothy 4:5-9.

Chapter 3—That little thing called body image

1. www.eatingdisorderscoalition.org/reports/statistics.html.
2. www.angie-jolie.com/quotes.html.
3. Michelle Graham, *Wanting to Be Her* (Downers Grove, IL: InterVarsity Press, 2005), 104.
4. See 1 Corinthians 6:19.
5. Lael Arrington, personal conversation with author.
6. Matthew Paul Turner, *Mind Games* (Wheaton, IL: Tyndale House Publishers, 2006).

7. Christine Hassler, *20-Something, 20-Everything* (Novato, CA: New World Library, 2005), 44.

Chapter 4—Love, marriage, and great sex

1. *Larry King Live,* "Bill Maher Discusses *Politically Incorrect,*" April 28, 2000.
2. Jason Illian, *Undressed: The Naked Truth About Love, Sex and Dating* (Brentwood, TN: FaithWords, 2006), 20.
3. Camerin Courtney and Todd Hertz, *The Unguide to Dating* (Grand Rapids, MI: Revell, 2006), 73.
4. Paris M. Finner-Williams, *Single Wisdom: Empowering Singles, Divorcees, Widows & Widowers for Living* (RP Publishings, 2005), 97.
5. Pam Farrel, personal conversation.
6. Shaunti Feldhahn and Lisa Rice, *For Young Women Only* (Sisters, OR: Multnomah, 2006), 10.

Chapter 5—The friendship factor

1. See Mark 14:32-40.
2. www.latimes.com/features/health/la-he-friends, 16ct.
3. www.latimes.com.
4. Julie Barnhill, "You Go, Gurlfriend!" talk.
5. Barnhill.
6. T. Suzanne Eller, *The Mom I Want to Be* (Eugene, OR: Harvest House, 2006), 114-115.

Chapter 6—Who is my community?

1. Margaret Feinberg, *Twentysomething* (Nashville, TN: W Publishing, 2004), 112.
2. Colin Creel, *Perspectives* (Orlando, FL: Relevant Books, 2005), p. iii.
3. Christine Hassler, *20-Something, 20-Everything: A Quarter-life Woman's Guide to Balance and Direction* (Novato, CA: New World Library, 2005), 100.
4. Kelly Monroe Kullberg, *Finding God Beyond Harvard* (Downers Grove, IL: InterVarsity Press, 2006), 92.
5. Matthew 18:20.
6. Proverbs 27:17.

Chapter 7—What is my faith story?

1. Jo Kadlecek, *Desperate Women of the Bible* (Grand Rapids, MI: Baker Books, 2006), p. 42.
2. See John 3:1-20.
3. John 3:16-17.
4. Matthew 27:51.
5. Galatians 2:16-19.
6. Galatians 2:20-21.
7. See Matthew 6:6-8.
8. Matthew 6:6.
9. Keri Wyatt Kent, *Listen: Finding God in the Story of Your Life* (Somerset, NJ: Jossey-Bass, 2006), 6.
10. Keri Wyatt Kent, personal conversation with the author.
11. Keri Wyatt Kent, personal conversation with the author.
12. Craig Groeschel, *Confessions of a Pastor* (Sisters, OR: Multnomah, 2006), 110.

Chapter 8—They say I'm called...to what?

1. Joanna Weaver, *Having a Mary Spirit* (Colorado Springs, CO: Waterbrook, 2006), 9.
2. James Martin, *My Life with the Saints* (Chicago: Loyola Press, 2006), 389-390.
3. John 14:26.
4. Esther 4:14.
5. Henry T. Blackaby and Norman C. Blackaby, *Called and Accountable,* rev. ed. (Birmingham, AL: New Hope Publishing, 2007), 61-62.
6. Weaver, 5.
7. Weaver, 23.

Chapter 9—Gucci or giving?

1. Leslie Vernick, *Selfless Joy in a Me-First World* (Colorado Springs, CO: Waterbrook, 2003), 23.
2. Facts About Children and Poverty, Care Organization, www.care.org/campaigns/childrenpoverty/facts.asp.
3. James 1:27.

4. Mark Allan Powell, *Giving to God: The Bible's Good News About Living a Generous Life* (Grand Rapids, MI: Wm. B. Eerdmans Publishing Company, 2006), xx.
5. See Mark 10:17-23.
6. Mark Allan Powell, "Giving to God, Interview with Mark Allan Powell, author of *Giving to God*," www.eerdmans.com/interviews/powellinterview.htm.
7. Gary Thomas, in foreword to Vernick, 1.
8. John 10:10.
9. Vernick, 4.

Chapter 10—Vocation—what is it? Why is it crucial?

1. Parker J. Palmer, *Let Your Life Speak* (Somerset, NJ: Jossey-Bass), 33.
2. 1 Corinthians 1:26-28.

Chapter 11—Changing the world

1. Used by permission.
2. John 13:34-35.
3. John 7:37-38.
4. See John 7:40-43.
5. John 7:38 NIV.

EXPLORING CHRISTIAN SPIRITUALITY

BECOMING WHO GOD INTENDED

A New Picture for Your Past • A Healthy Way of Managing Your Emotions • A Fresh Perspective on Relationships

David Eckman

Whether you realize it or not, your imagination is filled with *pictures* of reality. The Bible indicates these pictures reveal your true "heart beliefs"—the beliefs that actually shape your everyday feelings and reactions to family and friends, to your life circumstances, and to God.

David Eckman compassionately shows you how to allow God's Spirit to build new, *biblical* pictures in your heart and imagination. As you do this, you will be able to break free of negative emotions...and finally experience the life God has always intended for you.

SEX, FOOD, AND GOD

Breaking Free from Temptations, Compulsions, and Addictions

David Eckman

The good things created by God, like food and sex, can be misused to run away from emotional/relational pain. When this happens, the damage and loneliness can be worse than the worst nightmare.

Using groundbreaking research and offering compassionate understanding rooted deeply in the Bible, David Eckman shares

- how and why unhealthy appetites grip and trap people in a fantasy world
- how shame and guilt disappear when we realize how much God delights in us
- how four great experiences of the spiritual life break the addiction cycle

FROM FAKING IT TO FINDING GRACE

Discovering God Again When Your Faith Runs Dry

Connie Cavanaugh

Spiritual dryness and disillusionment—nobody ever talks about them. But the truth is, almost every believer experiences periods of feeling disconnected from God.

Writer and speaker Connie Cavanaugh speaks out of her own ten-year struggle. You can trust her to mentor you toward a deeper and more mature friendship with God. "You're not alone in this," she says, "so hold on to hope—He's calling you back."

FINDING A MENTOR, BEING A MENTOR

Sharing Our Lives as Women of God

Donna Otto

Not only does mentoring help you share the joys and pains of everyday life, it provides a place for you to discuss effective strategies to handle the demands of being a friend, wife, mother, student, or career woman. Bestselling author Donna Otto shows you how to develop and nourish a mentoring relationship that will help you...

- understand God's unique purpose for your life
- make better use of your time, skills, and spiritual gifts
- cultivate a stronger faith and trust in God

JUST MARRIED

What Might Surprise You About the First Few Years

Margaret Feinberg

Yep—you're married. You are no longer single and in sole possession of the remote, your finances, or your car. It helps to know how others have adjusted. Honest insights and stories from author Margaret Feinberg's own marriage and from others add reality to chapters such as...

- And Two Checkbooks Shall Become One?
- One More Time, Please. Why Do Opposites Attract?
- Oh, Baby—This Is Going to Change Our Life!
- Finding God (Again) After You've Found Your Mate
- What Do You Mean We Aren't the Only Two People in the World?

God planned marriage from the very beginning. As you look to Him, He will help you and your new spouse successfully embark on the incredible adventure of wedded life.

LIFE, LIBBY, AND THE PURSUIT OF HAPPINESS
Hope Lyda

Here's the urban tale of Libby Marshall, whose life seems to be going the wrong direction. She creates trip itineraries but never travels. She wants to attend church but winds up at a bookstore on Sundays. She longs for a love attraction yet settles for a "like" distraction.

But when Libby receives a demotion instead of her overdue promotion, she vows to start living intentionally. Yet just when she is trying to be authentic, she is asked to keep a huge secret to redeem her career. Will a genuine life ever be within reach? And will Libby ever have enough faith to believe that happiness can be found in the detours?

THE CUBICLE NEXT DOOR
Siri Mitchell

Jackie Harrison loves her job at the U.S. Air Force Academy—until she is forced to divide her office into cubicles and share the space with Lt. Col. Joseph Gallagher, a charmer in a flight suit who wants to explore a growing relationship with his new cubicle mate.

Jackie goes online to vent. Eventually, though, she finds herself admitting that her office neighbor both drives her crazy...and makes her heart flutter. But then her blog—The Cubicle Next Door—is featured on TV. Everyone begins to read it, including Joe. Will he figure out the anonymous confessions and frustrations are written about him? And how will Jackie come clean about her feelings?

MOON OVER TOKYO
Siri Mitchell

Though reporter Allie O'Connor has lived in Japan for two years, as a foreigner she still barely copes. After an office romance ends badly and she's left lonely, she prays one moonlit night for a friend. *Just a friend.*

Soon after, at church, she runs into an old classmate from high school. Eric Larson has been assigned to the U.S. Embassy and lives in Allie's district in Tokyo. In school he had been a young Republican, she a liberal Democrat. He drank espresso, she preferred green tea. Definitely *not* the friend she was looking for. And yet, now that they are grown up, they find they have some things in common. Perhaps more than they first realize...